Table of Contents
(Publication Date – March 2013)

Introduction..v

Acknowledgements vi

Assault Weapons...1
    Myth: Assault weapons are a serious problem in the U.S. 1
    Myth: Every 48 hours, an assault rifle is traced to crime in Maryland....................... 2
    Myth: One out of five police officers killed are killed with assault weapons 3
    Myth: Assault weapons are favored by criminals.. 3
    Myth: Assault weapons can be easily converted to machine guns 3
    Myth: Assault weapons are used in 16% of homicides 4
    Myth: The 1994 (former) Federal Assault Weapons Ban was effective 4
    Myth: Nobody needs an assault weapon.. 5

The availability of guns 7
    Myth: The availability of guns causes crime 7
    Myth: Gun availability is what is causing school shootings....................................... 9
    Myth: Gun availability leads to massacres 9
    Myth: Gun ownership is linked to higher homicide rates.. 9
    Myth: Handguns are 43 times more likely to kill a family member than a criminal............... 10

Children and guns..11
    Myth: 13 children are killed each day by guns... 11
    Myth: School yard shootings are an epidemic... 12
    Myth: Trigger locks will keep children from accidentally shooting themselves...... 13
    Myth: Guns in America spark youth violence 13
    Myth: More than 1,300 children commit suicide with guns 14
    Myth: Stricter gun control laws could have prevented the Columbine massacre...... 15
    Myth: Children should be kept away from guns for their own safety 15
    Myth: More children are hurt with guns than by any other means........................... 15
    Myth: If it saves the life of one child, it is worth it 16

Accidental deaths 19
    Myth: Accidental gun fatalities are a serious problem 19
    Myth: Handguns are unsafe and cause accidents... 20
    Myth: Innocent bystanders are often killed by guns.. 21
    Myth: Citizens are too incompetent to use guns for protection............................... 21
    Myth: Gun accidents are flooding emergency rooms... 21
    Myth: "Junk" guns are dangerous and should be banned 21
    Myth: Guns should be made to conform to product liability laws 21

Concealed carry laws and weapons...23
    Myth: Concealed carry doesn't prevent crimes 23

Gun Facts Version 6.2   Page i
Copyright 2013, Guy Smith   www.GunFacts.info   All Rights Reserved

INTRODUCTION

> "The great enemy of the truth is very often not the lie: deliberate, continued, and dishonest; but the myth: persistent, persuasive, and unrealistic."
>
> -- John F. Kennedy

Purpose

The goal of *Gun Facts* is to provide a quick reference guide for civil libertarians on gun control issues. Use *Gun Facts* when composing arguments for debates, writing letters to editors, emailing to your representatives, and sending statements to the media.

The problem *Gun Facts* addresses is the lack of intellectual honesty by gun control advocates. Over many decades they have presented "information" to the media and the public that is at best inaccurate and at worst fraudulent. *Gun Facts* is dedicated to debunking gun control myths and providing citable evidence.

Common gun control myths are listed in the pages that follow. For each myth, one or more facts are presented to refute the gun control claim and the source of the information is fully cited.

Copyright and free usage information

This work is the copyrighted property of Guy Smith. All rights are reserved unless noted below.

PDF: The PDF version of this document may be freely distributed providing the document is not altered and that the source is always cited. "Reasonable use" laws apply, which basically means you can use small sections of *Gun Facts* without my prior consent. Written excerpts may be distributed as long as the URL 'www.GunFacts.info' is identified as the location where the full document may be obtained.

Printings: You are also allowed to print this document for your personal reference and/or for distribution without fee (i.e., you can't charge money for copies of *Gun Facts*). This means if you want to print copies for the media, elected officials, gun shows, friends, etc. – you are free to do so. Any distribution in any format must include the entire work.

Questions, corrections and suggestions

If you need to communicate with the author, send e-mail to guy@GunFacts.info. Your corrections, comments, additions and suggestions are welcomed and encouraged. When providing new information, please cite the original reference in detail – publication, title, author, date, etc. This is essential.

Sources

All sources cited in this work are accurate to the best of my research. I use the most recent data I can easily find and I have time to update. If any more recent data is available (even if it weakens my arguments), I welcome receiving the same.

Contributions

I accept non-tax-exempt donations to pay for the software, hardware, paper and ink used in composing, editing and distributing *Gun Facts*. If you would like to help, drop by www.PayPal.com and send your donations to guy@GunFacts.info.

Printed copies

A printed copy of the current version of *Gun Facts* can be acquired online at Amazon.com.

ACKNOWLEDGEMENTS

My sincere thanks go out to the following individuals or groups for their contributions to *Gun Facts*:

Jim Archer: Long ago Jim provided the domain www.GunFacts.info, so people can more easily find this work.

Skeff: For handling a bunch of IT work and building the online core of the Gun Facts community.

Proofers: Thanks also to Dale, Randy, Steve, Bob, Andrea, Chad, Ron, Eric, The Other Bob, Stace, Woody, Keith, TC, Paul, Gary, Darren, Sherre, Christopher, Mark, Joe, Mike, Augustin, Michael, The Third Bob, David, Mark The Second, Jack, Neva, Liam, Earl, Doug and Phil who volunteered to proofread this version of *Gun Facts* and thus obscured my own inabilities.

Pete McKay/McKayDesign: For the very professional front cover design.

Muchas gracias: Thank you Claudia, Gonzalo, Renzo, Pablo, Cecilia, Malcolm and Ignacio for the first translation of Gun Facts into Spanish.

The Research Volunteers: Over 600 people have registered to help in researching topics and specific items. I cannot list every volunteer, so I thank you collectively.

Jason G.: For originally recommending the myth/fact approach, which has proven to be absolutely the right way to present this information.

Shooting The Bull

By Gun Facts author, Guy Smith

In politics, everyone lies. Voters distrust everything they are told by politicians, the media and even their neighbors. Despite universal suspicion of news and opinion makers, very few people understand how political lies are created and thus most folk are unable to dissect spin and discover truth. *Shooting the Bull* details how all political falsehoods are created, why they work and how to detect them.

Nowhere on the political landscape are more lies told than within the churning bowels of the gun control industry. Fighting America's revolutionary reluctance to submit and the public's continuing fear of criminals not currently incarcerated in Congress, voters have resisted legislative agendas proposed by The Brady Campaign, Violence Policy Center and the Clinton administration. For decades, significant victories have eluded their ilk, leaving only one strategy with which to sway voters – lying.

Shooting the Bull serves two purposes. First, it catalogs the common canards of politicians and activists. Readers will recognize how they have been psychologically scammed by special interests and deceived by elected sycophants. They will also experience disquieting revelations as they discover forms of fibs they had previously encountered but not recognized. By the end of the book, readers will be infinitely more cynical about politicians and propagandists and be equipped to dissect future electoral effluvium.

The second purpose of *Shooting the Bull* is to document the deceits peddled by the gun control lobby. Each chapter is devoted to at least one major initiative proffered by anti-gun activists, exposing their falsities through dissection of their motives, methods and inconvenient facts. The art and science of political pretense is illustrated through Senator Dianne Feinstein's "assault weapon" ban, the Million Mom March's campaign to register all guns and license all owners, and Michael Moore's deluded "documentaries"

Buy Today at Amazon.com

ASSAULT WEAPONS

"Assault weapon" is an invented term. In the firearm lexicon, there is no such thing as an "assault weapon."[1] The closest relative is the "assault rifle," which is a machine gun or "select fire" rifle that fires rifle cartridges.[2] In most cases, "assault weapons" are functionally identical though less powerful than hunting rifles, but they are cosmetically similar to military guns.

MYTH: ASSAULT WEAPONS ARE A SERIOUS PROBLEM IN THE U.S.

Fact: In 1994, before the Federal "assault weapons ban," you were eleven (11) times more likely to be beaten to death than to be killed by an "assault weapon."[3]

Fact: In the first year since the ban was lifted, murders declined 3.6%, and violent crime 1.7%.[4]

Fact: Nationally, "assault weapons" were used in 1.4% of crimes involving firearms and 0.25% of all violent crime before the enactment of any national or state "assault weapons" ban. In many major urban areas (San Antonio, Mobile, Nashville, etc.) and some entire states (Maryland, New Jersey, etc.) the rate is less than 0.1%.[5]

Fact: Even weapons misclassified as "assault weapons" (common in the former Federal and California "assault weapons" confiscations) are used in less than 1% of all homicides.[6]

Fact: Police reports show that "assault weapons" are a non-problem:

For California:

- **Los Angeles:** In 1998, of 538 documented gun incidents, only one (0.2%) involved an "assault weapon."
- **San Francisco:** In 1998, only 2.2% of confiscated weapons were "assault weapons."
- **San Diego:** Between 1988 and 1990, only 0.3% of confiscated weapons were "assault weapons."
- "I surveyed the firearms used in violent crimes...assault-type firearms were the least of our worries."[7]

---

[1] It is worth noting that there are numerous different 'legal' definitions of "assault weapons". A report from the Legal Community Against Violence showed no fewer than eight jurisdictions, anywhere from 19 to 75 banned firearms, six differing generic classification schemes and several legal systems for banning more firearms without specific legislative action. In other words, an "assault weapon" is whatever a politician deems it to be.

[2] *Small Arms Identification and Operations Guide*, U.S. Department of Defense. The exact statement from their manual is "short, compact, select-fire weapons that fires a cartridge intermediate in power between submachine gun and rifle cartridges."

[3] FBI Uniform Crime Statistics, 1994

[4] FBI Uniform Crime Statistics, Preliminary Summary, 2004

[5] *Targeting Guns*, Gary Kleck, Aldine Transaction, 1997, compilation of 48 metropolitan police departments from 1980-1994

[6] FBI Uniform Crime Statistics, 1993

[7] S.C. Helsley, Assistant Director DOJ Investigation and Enforcement Branch, California, October 31, 1988

For the rest of the nation:

- Between 1980 and 1994, only 2% of confiscated guns were "assault weapons."[8]
- Just under 2% of criminals that commit violent crimes used "assault weapons."[9]

Fact: Only 1.4% of recovered crime weapons are models covered under the 1994 "assault weapons" ban.[10]

Fact: In Virginia, no surveyed inmates had carried an "assault weapon" during the commission of their last crime, despite 20% admitting that they had previously owned such weapons.[11]

Fact: Most "assault weapons" have no more firepower or killing capacity than the average hunting rifle and "play a small role in overall violent crime."[12]

Fact: Even the government agrees. "... the weapons banned by this legislation [1994 Federal Assault Weapons ban - since repealed] were used only rarely in gun crimes"[13]

Myth: Every 48 hours, an assault rifle is traced to crime in Maryland

Fact: This claim by Cease Fire Maryland includes firearms never used in crimes. Some examples of firearms traced include:

> "No one should have any illusions about what was accomplished (by the ban). Assault weapons play a part in only a small percentage of crime. The provision is mainly symbolic; its virtue will be if it turns out to be, as hoped, a stepping stone to broader gun control."
>
> Washington Post editorial
> September 15, 1994

- 47 firearms found at private residence of a person who passed-away from natural causes, and which were never used in any crime.

- Firearms temporarily taken from owners under court Emergency Evaluation Petitions (the firearms were not used in crimes, but the judge wanted them confiscated until other issues are resolved).

Fact: This claim lacks perspective. During the same time period there were 163,101 violent crimes reported in Maryland. Even if the Cease Fire Maryland data was correct, they have connected assault rifles to just 0.4% of violent crimes during the same period.

---

[8] *Targeting Guns*, Gary Kleck, Aldine Transaction, 1997, compilation of 48 metropolitan police departments from 1980-1994

[9] *Targeting Guns*, Gary Kleck, Aldine Transaction, 1997, calculated from Bureau of Justice Statistics, assault weapon recovery rates

[10] From statewide recovery report from Connecticut (1988-1993) and Pennsylvania (1989-1994)

[11] Criminal Justice Research Center, Department of Criminal Justice Services, 1994

[12] *House Panel Issue: Can Gun Ban Work*, New York Times. April 7, 1989. P. A-15, quoting Philip McGuire, Handgun Control, Inc.,

[13] *Impacts of the 1994 Assault Weapons Ban: 1994-96*, National Institute of Justice, March 1999

Myth: One out of five police officers killed are killed with assault weapons[14]

Fact: This "study" included firearms not on the former Federal "assault weapons" list. Including various legal firearms[15] inflated the statistics almost 100%.

Fact: Only 1% of police officers murdered were killed using "assault weapons." They were twice as likely to be killed with their own handgun.[16]

Fact: One 2006 federal government study found *zero* "assault weapons" were used to kill police officers.[17]

Myth: Assault weapons are favored by criminals

Fact: Only 6% of criminals use anything that is classified (even incorrectly) as an "assault weapon,"[18] though less than 2.5% claimed to use these firearms when committing crimes.[19]

Fact: Criminals are over five times more likely to carry single shot handguns as they are to carry "assault weapons."[20]

Fact: "Assault rifles have never been an issue in law enforcement. I have been on this job for 25 years and I haven't seen a drug dealer carry one. They are not used in crimes, they are not used against police officers."[21]

Fact: "Since police started keeping statistics, we now know that 'assault weapons' are/were used in an underwhelming 0.026 of 1% of crimes in New Jersey. This means that my officers are more likely to confront an escaped tiger from the local zoo than to confront an assault rifle in the hands of a drug-crazed killer on the streets."[22]

Thoughts: "Assault weapons" are large and unwieldy. Even misclassified handguns tend to be bigger than practical for concealed carry. Criminals (who, incidentally, disregard concealed carry laws) are unlikely to carry "assault weapons."

Myth: Assault weapons can be easily converted to machine guns

Fact: Firearms that can be "readily converted" are already prohibited by law.[23]

---

[14] This claim was made by the anti-gun Violence Policy Center in their 2003 report titled *Officer Down*

[15] The "study" included legal models of the SKS, Ruger Mini-14, and M1-Carbine, which were all in circulation before the federal "assault weapons" ban and which were excluded from the ban.

[16] *Law Enforcement Officers Killed and Assaulted*, FBI, 1994

[17] *Violent Encounters: A Study of Felonious Assaults on Our Nation's Law Enforcement Officers*, U.S. Department of Justice, August 2006

[18] *Firearm Use by Offenders* , Bureau of Justice Statistics, November 2001

[19] Ibid.

[20] Ibid

[21] Deputy Chief of Police Joseph Constance, Trenton NJ, testimony - Senate Judiciary Committee in Aug 1993

[22] Ibid

[23] U.S. Code title 26, subtitle E, Chapter 53, subchapter B, part 1, section 5845

Fact: None of the firearms on the list of banned weapons can be readily converted.[24]

Fact: Only 0.15% of over 4,000 weapons confiscated in Los Angeles in one year were converted, and only 0.3% had any evidence of an attempt to convert.[25]

MYTH: ASSAULT WEAPONS ARE USED IN 16% OF HOMICIDES

Fact: This figure was concocted to promote an "assault weapons" bill in New York. Their classification scheme included most firearms sold in the U.S. since 1987 (center fire rifles, shotguns holding more than six cartridges, and handguns holding more than 10 rounds). By misclassifying most firearms as "assault weapons," they expanded the scope of a non-problem.

> "Passing a law like the assault weapons ban is a symbolic, purely symbolic move ... Its only real justification is not to reduce crime but to desensitize the public to the regulation of weapons in preparation for their ultimate confiscation."
>
> Charles Krauthammer, Syndicated Columnist, The Washington Post April 5, 1996

MYTH: THE 1994 (FORMER) FEDERAL ASSAULT WEAPONS BAN WAS EFFECTIVE

Fact: " ... we cannot clearly credit the ban with any of the nation's recent drop in gun violence."[26]

Fact: The ban covered only 1.39% of the models of firearms on the market, so the ban's effectiveness is automatically limited.

Fact: "The ban has failed to reduce the average number of victims per gun murder incident or multiple gunshot wound victims."[27]

Fact: "The public safety benefits of the 1994 ban have not yet been demonstrated."[28]

Fact: "The ban triggered speculative price increases and ramped-up production of the banned firearms."[29]

Fact: "The ban ... ramped-up production of the banned firearms prior to the law's implementation"[30] and thus increased the total supply over the following decade.

---

[24] BATF test as reported in the New York Times, April 3, 1989

[25] Congressional testimony, Jimmy Trahin, Los Angeles Detective, Subcommittee on the Constitution of the Committee on the Judiciary, May 5, 1989, 101st Congress, 1st Session, Washington, DC, US Government Printing Office, May 5, 1989, p. 379

[26] *An Updated Assessment of the Federal Assault Weapons Ban: Impacts on Gun Markets and Gun Violence, 1994-2003*, National Institute of Justice, June 2004

[27] *Impacts of the 1994 Assault Weapons Ban: 1994-96*, National Institute of Justice, March 1999

[28] Ibid

[29] Ibid

[30] Ibid

Fact: The Brady Campaign claims that "After the 1994 ban, there were 18% fewer 'assault weapons' traced to crime in the first eight months of 1995 than were traced in the same period in 1994." However they failed to note (and these are mentioned in the NIJ study) that:

1. "Assault weapons" traces were minimal before the ban (due to their infrequent use in crimes), so an 18% change enters the realm of statistical irrelevancy.

2. Fewer "assault weapons" were available to criminals because collectors bought-up the available supply before the ban.

MYTH: NOBODY NEEDS AN ASSAULT WEAPON

Fact: Their light weight and durability make them suitable for many types of hunting and are especially favored for wild boar hunting.

Fact: Recall the Rodney King riots in that anti-gun city of Los Angeles. Every major news network carried footage of Korean storeowners sitting on the roofs of their stores, armed with "assault weapons."[31] Those were the stores that did ***not*** get burned to the ground, and those were the people that were ***not*** dragged into the street and beaten by rioters. "You can't get around the image of people shooting at people to protect their stores and it working. This is damaging to the [gun control] movement."[32]

Fact: There are many reasons people prefer to use these firearms:

- They are easy to operate
- They are very reliable in outdoor conditions (backpacking, hunting, etc.)
- They are accurate
- They are good for recreational and competitive target shooting
- They have value in many self-defense situations

Fact: There are many sports in which these firearms are required:

- Many hunters use these firearms (especially for wild boar hunting in the south)
- Three-gun target matches
- Camp Perry competitions, especially the Service Rifle events
- DCM/CMP competitions
- Bodyguard simulations

Fact: Ours is a Bill of <u>Rights</u>, not a Bill of <u>Needs</u>.

---

[31] Washington Post, May 2, 1992

[32] Josh Sugarmann, executive director of the Violence Policy Center, Washington Post, May 18, 1993

THE AVAILABILITY OF GUNS

MYTH: THE AVAILABILITY OF GUNS CAUSES CRIME

Fact: Though the number of firearms owned by private citizens has been increasing steadily since 1970, the overall rate of homicides and suicides has not risen.[33] As the chart shows, there is no correlation between the availability of firearms and the rates of homicide and suicide in America.

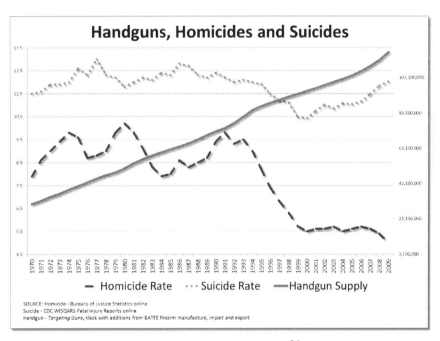

Handguns, Homicides and Suicides

— Homicide Rate   ··· Suicide Rate   ═══Handgun Supply

SOURCE: Homicide - Bureau of Justice Statistics online
Suicide - CDC WISQARS Fatal Injury Reports online
Handgun - *Targeting Guns*, Kleck with additions from BATFE firearm manufacture, import and export

Fact: Internationally speaking "There's no clear relationship between more guns and higher levels of violence."[34]

Fact: "A detailed study of the major surveys completed in the past 20 years or more provides no evidence of any relationship between the total number of legally held firearms in society and the rate of armed crime. Nor is there a relationship between the severity of controls imposed in various countries or the mass of bureaucracy involved with many control systems with the apparent ease of access to firearms by criminals and terrorists."[35]

Fact: Handgun ownership among groups normally associated with higher violent crime (young males, blacks, low income, inner city, etc.) is at or below national averages.[36]

Fact: Among inmates who used a firearm in the commission of a crime, the most significant correlations occurred when the inmates' parents abused drugs (27.5%) and when inmates had friends engaged in illegal activities (32.5% for robberies, 24.3% for drug trafficking)." [37]

---

[33], *Targeting Guns: Firearms and Their Control*, Gary Kleck, Aldine de Gruyter, 1997. (With supporting data from the FBI Uniform Crime Statistics, 1972 to 1995.)

[34] *Small Arms Survey Project*, Keith Krause, Graduate Institute of International Studies, Geneva, 2007

[35] *Minutes of Evidence*, Colin Greenwood, Select Committee on Northern Ireland Affairs, January 29, 2003

[36] *Targeting Guns: Firearms and Their Control*, Gary Kleck, Aldine de Gruyter, 1997. (Ownership tables derived from the annual "General Social Survey.")

[37] *Firearm Use by Offenders*, Bureau of Justice Statistics, November 2001

Fact: Five out of six gun-possessing felons obtained handguns from the secondary market and by theft, and "[the] criminal handgun market is overwhelmingly dominated by informal transactions and theft as mechanisms of supply."[38]

Fact: The majority of handguns in the possession of criminals are stolen, and not necessarily by the criminals in question.[39] In fact, over 100,000 firearms are stolen in burglaries every year, and most of them likely enter the criminal market (i.e., are sold or traded to criminals).[40]

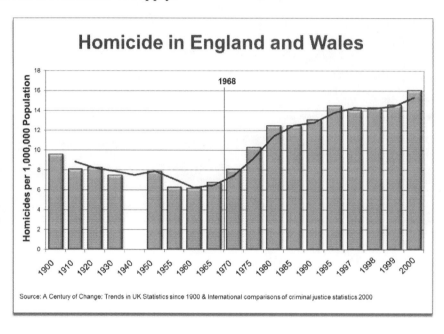

Homicide in England and Wales

Source: A Century of Change: Trends in UK Statistics since 1900 & International comparisons of criminal justice statistics 2000

Fact: In 1968, the U.K. passed laws that reduced the number of licensed firearm owners, and thus reduced firearm availability. U.K. homicide rates **have steadily risen** since then.[41] Ironically, firearm use in crimes has *doubled* in the decade after the U.K. banned handguns.[42]

Fact: Most violent crime is caused by a small minority of repeat offenders. One California study found that 3.8% of a group of males born in 1956 were responsible for 55.5% of all serious felonies.[43] 75-80% of murder arrestees have prior arrests for a violent (including non-fatal) felony or burglary. On average they have about four felony arrests and one felony conviction.

---

[38] *The Armed Criminal in America: A Survey of Incarcerated Felons*, James D. Wright, Peter H. Rossi, National Institute of Justice (U.S.), 1985

[39] *Targeting Guns: Firearms and Their Control,* Gary Kleck, Aldine de Gruyter, 1997.

[40] *Victimization During Household Burglary*, Bureau of Justice Statistics, September 2010

[41] *A Century of Change: Trends in UK Statistics since 1900*, Hicks, Joe; Allen, Grahame (SGS), Social and General Statistics Section, House of Commons

[42] *Weapons sell for just £50 as suspects and victims grow ever younger*, The Times, August 24, 2007

[43] *The Prevalence and Incidence of Arrest Among Adult Males in California*, Robert Tillman, prepared for California Department of Justice, Bureau of Criminal Statistics and Special Services, Sacramento, California, 1987

Fact: Half of all murders are committed by people on "conditional release" (i.e., parole or probation).[44] 81% of all homicide defendants had an arrest record; 67% had a felony arrest record; 70% had a conviction record; and 54% had a felony conviction.[45]

Fact: Per capita firearm ownership rates have risen steadily since 1959 while crime rates have gone up and down depending on economics, drug trafficking innovations, and "get tough" legislation.[46]

Thoughts: Criminals are not motivated by guns. They are motivated by opportunity. Attempts to reduce public access to firearms provide criminals more points of opportunity. It is little wonder that high-crime cities also tend to be those with the most restrictive gun control laws – which criminals tend to ignore.

MYTH: GUN AVAILABILITY IS WHAT IS CAUSING SCHOOL SHOOTINGS

Fact: Schoolyard shootings have been occurring since at least 1974, so it is not a new phenomenon due to increases in gun ownership.[47]

Fact: More than 50% of these terrorists started thinking about their assaults two or more weeks before the shooting, and 75% planned-out their attacks.[48]

Thoughts: In rural areas, guns are everywhere and children are taught to shoot at young ages – yet these areas are almost devoid of schoolyard shootings. Clearly, availability is not the issue.

MYTH: GUN AVAILABILITY LEADS TO MASSACRES

Fact: In 62% of mass public shootings, the assailant had a history of "displayed signs of mental health problems prior to the killings."[49]

MYTH: GUN OWNERSHIP IS LINKED TO HIGHER HOMICIDE RATES

Fact: This "study"[50] has multiple defects which, when corrected, reverse the results. Some of the defects of this study include:

* Exclusion of the District of Columbia, a high crime city

---

[44] *Probation and Parole Violators in State Prison, 1991: Survey of State Prison Inmates*, Robyn Cohen, U.S. Dept. of Justice, Office of Justice Programs, Bureau of Justice Statistics, 1995

[45] *Felony Defendants in Large Urban Counties, 1998*, Brian Reaves, U.S. Department of Justice, Office of Justice Programs, Bureau of Justice Statistics, November 2001

[46] Ibid. (Based on a compilation of 85 separate surveys from 1959 through 1996.)

[47] *U.S.S.S. Safe School Initiative: An Interim Report on the Prevention of Targeted Violence in Schools*, B. Vossekuil, M. Reddy, R. Fein, R. Borum, & W. Modzeleski, U. S. Secret Service, Threat Assessment Center, 2000

[48] Ibid.

[49] *Mass Shootings: Maybe What We Need Is a Better Mental-Health Policy*, Mother Jones, November 9, 2012

[50] *State-level homicide victimization rates in the US in relation to survey measures of household firearm ownership, 2001–2003*, Matthew Miller, David Hemenwaya, Deborah Azrael, Harvard School of Public Health, October 27, 2006

- Use of other crime rates to indirectly explain homicide rates

- Use of purely cross-sectional data that never allows control variable analysis

- Data from different years is used without any explanation (unemployment rate from 2000 to explain the homicide rate from 2001 to 2003, etc.).

MYTH: HANDGUNS ARE 43 TIMES MORE LIKELY TO KILL A FAMILY MEMBER THAN A CRIMINAL

Fact: Of the 43 deaths reported in this flawed study, 37 (86%) were suicides. Other deaths involved criminal activity between the family members (drug deals gone bad).[51]

Fact: Of the remaining deaths, the deceased family members include felons, drug dealers, violent spouses committing assault, and other criminals.[52]

Fact: Only 0.1% of the defensive uses of guns results in the death of the predator.[53] This means you are much more likely to <u>prevent a crime without bloodshed</u> than hurt a family member.

---

[51] *Protection or Peril? An Analysis of Firearm-Related Deaths in the Home*, Arthur L. Kellerman, D.T. Reay, 314 New Eng. J. Med. 1557-60, June 12, 1986. (Kellerman admits that his study did "not include cases in which burglars or intruders are wounded or frightened away by the use or display of a firearm." He also admitted his study did not look at situations in which intruders "purposely avoided a home known to be armed." This is a classic case of a "study" conducted to achieve a desired result. In his critique of this "study", Gary Kleck notes that the estimation of gun ownership rates was "inaccurate", and that the total population came from a non-random selection of only two cities.)

[52] Ibid.

[53] *Point Blank: Guns and Violence in America*, Gary Kleck, New York: Aldine de Gruyter, 1991

CHILDREN AND GUNS

MYTH: 13 CHILDREN ARE KILLED EACH DAY BY GUNS

Fact: Adults included – This "statistic" includes "children" up to age 19 or 24, depending on the source.[54] Most violent crime is committed by males ages 16-24, these numbers end up including adult gang members dying during criminal activity. The proper definition of 'child' is a person between birth and puberty (typically 13-14 years old).

Fact: 301 children (age 14 and under) died from gunfire in all of 2010 or less than one per day. This includes homicides, accidents, and suicides combined.[55]

Fact: Criminals are included - According to the CDC, over half of all homicides of victims aged 15-19 are gang-related. The same study found that gang-related homicides are more likely to involve firearms than those that are not (95% versus 69%).[56]

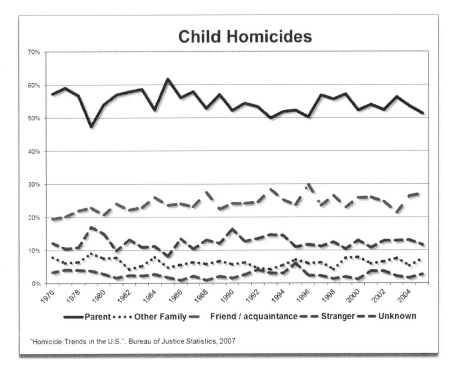

"Homicide Trends in the U.S.", Bureau of Justice Statistics, 2007

Fact: Suicides are included – 27% of child firearm deaths are suicides. - These numbers include suicides.[57][58]

Fact: The federal government lists the total firearm related deaths for children at 301, or less than one per day, in 2010. 81 were suicides.[59]

---

[54] Center for Disease Control WISQARS Fatal Injury Reports for 2010

[55] Ibid

[56] CDC Morbidity and Mortality Weekly Report: "Gang Homicides -- Five U.S. Cities, 2003-2008", published January 27, 2012

[57] *Rates of Homicide, Suicide, and Firearm-Related Death Among Children – 26 Industrialized Countries* National Center for Health Statistics, 1997

[58] Center for Disease Control WISQARS Fatal Injury Reports for 2010

[59] Ibid

Fact: Four children die every day in automobiles.[60]

Fact: Four children die each day in the U.S. from parental neglect and abuse.[61]

Fact: For contrast: 1,917 children die each day from malaria[62] around the world and 15 men, women, and children per day are murdered by a convicted felon in government supervised parole/probation programs in the U.S.[63]

MYTH: SCHOOL YARD SHOOTINGS ARE AN EPIDEMIC

Fact: "Compared to other types of violence and crime children face, both in and outside of school, school-based attacks are rare. While the Department of Education reports 60 million children attend the nation's 119,000 schools, available statistics indicate that few of these students will fall prey to violent situations in school settings".[64]

Fact: Over an eight year period, instates without "right to carry" laws, there were 15 school shootings; however, in states that allow citizens to carry guns, there was only one.[65]

Fact: The five school shootings that occurred during the '97-98 school year took place after the 1995 Gun-Free School Zones law was enacted, which banned guns within 1,000 feet of a school.[66]

Fact: Schoolyard shooting deaths are not rising, rather, they have been falling through most of the 1990s:[67]

Schoolyard Shootings	
1992-93	**55** deaths
1993-94	**51** deaths
1994-95	**20** deaths
1995-96	**35** deaths
1996-97	**25** deaths
1997-98	**40** deaths

Fact: Only 10% of public schools reported one or more serious violent crimes during the 1996-97 school year.[68]

Fact: In Pearl, Mississippi, the assistant principal carried a firearm to the school until the 1995 "Gun-Free School Zones" law passed. Afterwards he began locking his firearm in his car and parking at least a quarter-mile away from the school. In 1997, when a student began a shooting rampage, the assistant principal ran to his car, got his gun, ran back, disarmed the shooter and held him on the ground until the police arrived. Had the law not been passed, the assistant principal might have prevented the two deaths and seven shooting-related injuries.

Fact: Similar preventions occurred at a school dance in Edinboro, Pennsylvania, the Appalachian School of Law and during classes in Santee, California.

---

[60] Ibid

[61] National Center on Child Abuse Prevention, 1998 Annual Survey

[62] *Fact Sheet No 178*, U.N. World Health Organization, 1998

[63] US Bureau of Justice Statistics, 1998

[64] *Threat Assessment in Schools*, U.S. Secret Service and U.S. Department of Education, May 2002

[65] *Multiple Victim Public Shootings, Bombings, and Right-to-Carry Concealed Handgun Laws: Contrasting Private and Public Law Enforcement*, Lott J, Landes W; ,University of Chicago – (covers years 1977 to 1995)

[66] Ibid

[67] *Violence and Discipline Problems in U.S. Public Schools*, National Center for Education Statistics, 1996-97

[68] *Principal/School Disciplinarian Survey on School Violence*, Department of Education, March, 2000

MYTH: TRIGGER LOCKS WILL KEEP CHILDREN FROM ACCIDENTALLY SHOOTING THEMSELVES

Fact: 31 of 32 models of gun locks tested by the government's Consumer Product Safety Commission could be opened without the key. According to their spokesperson, "We found you could open locks with paper clips, a pair of scissors or tweezers, or you could whack them on the table and they would open."[69]

Fact: 85% of all communities in America recorded no juvenile homicides in 1995, and 93.4% of communities recorded one or no juvenile arrests (not convictions) for murder.[70]

Fact: In 1996, before before laws requiring trigger locks and when there were around 80 million people who owned a firearm, there were only 44 accidental gun deaths for children under age 10, or about 0.0001%.[71]

Fact: California has a trigger lock law and saw a 12% <u>increase</u> in fatal firearm accidents in 1994. Texas doesn't have one and experienced a 28% <u>decrease</u> in the same year.[72] Also: trigger-locks render a firearm inaccessible for timely self-defense.

Fact: Children as young as seven (7) years old have demonstrated that they can pick or break a trigger lock; or that they can operate a gun with a trigger lock in place.[73] Over half of non-criminal firearm deaths for children over age seven are suicides, so trigger locks are unlikely to reduce these deaths.

Fact: If criminals are deterred from attacking victims because of the fear that people might be able to defend themselves, gunlocks may in turn *reduce the danger to criminals* committing crime, and thus increase crime. This problem is exacerbated because many mechanical locks (such as barrel or trigger locks) also require that the gun be stored unloaded.

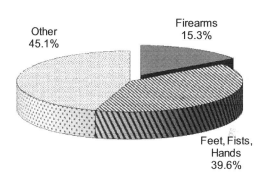

Homicide Weapons (victims under 13)

Other 45.1%

Firearms 15.3%

Feet, Fists, Hands 39.6%

MYTH: GUNS IN AMERICA SPARK YOUTH VIOLENCE

Fact: Non-firearm juvenile violent crime rate in the U.S. is twice that of 25 other industrialized western nations. The non-firearm infant-homicide rate in the U.S. is 3.5 times higher.[74] Thus we have a violence problem – not a "gun" problem.

---

[69] Washington Post, Feb 7, 2001, Page A01

[70] *Crime in the United States: Uniform Crime Reports*, Federal Bureau of Investigation, 1996

[71] CBS News web site,Prof. John Lott, March 20, 2000

[72] National Center for Health Statistics, 1995

[73] *Accidental Shootings: many deaths and injuries caused by firearms could be prevented*,United States General Accounting Office, March 1991

[74] *Kids and Guns* Bulletin, Centers for Disease Control and Prevention statistics, 2000. (Covers years 1990-1995)

Fact: Non-firearm related homicides of children out-rank firearm related homicides by children almost 5-to-1[75]

MYTH: MORE THAN 1,300 CHILDREN COMMIT SUICIDE WITH GUNS

Fact: This statistic includes "children" ages 18-19.[76] As established previously, a child is defined as a person between birth and the age of 13 or 14 (puberty).

Fact: Worldwide, the per capita suicide rate is fairly static (the suicide rate of the U.S. is lower than many industrial countries, including many where private gun ownership is banned). A certain fraction of the population will commit suicide regardless of the available tools.

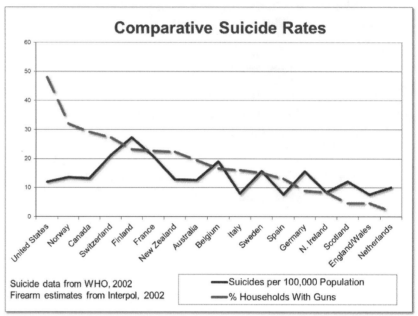

Comparative Suicide Rates

Suicide data from WHO, 2002
Firearm estimates from Interpol, 2002

—— Suicides per 100,000 Population
- - - % Households With Guns

Fact: The overall rate of suicide (firearm and non-firearm) among children age 15 and under was virtually unchanged in states that passed and maintained "safe storage" laws for four or more years.[77]

Fact: Among young girls, 71% of all suicides are by hanging or suffocation.[78]

Fact: People, including children, who are determined to commit suicide will find a way. There is a documented case of a man who killed himself by drilling a hole in his skull by using a power drill.[79]

Fact: Banning country music might be more effective – one study shows 51% of the music-influenced suicide differential can be traced to country music.[80]

---

[75] FBI Uniform Crime Statistics, 1997

[76] Determined using CDC mortality data, and finding the only possible fit for the claim.

[77] *Accidental Deaths, Suicides, and Crime Safe Storage Gun Laws*, John Lott, Yale Law School, 2000

[78] *Suicide Trends Among Youths and Young Adults Aged 10--24 Years --- United States, 1990--2004*, Center for Disease Control, September, 2007

[79] *Drilled Head Husband Dies in Hospital*, The Scotsman, April 28, 2003

[80] *The Effect of Country Music on Suicide*, Steven Stack, Jim Gundlach, Social Forces. Volume: 71. Issue: 1., 1992

Myth: Stricter gun control laws could have prevented the Columbine massacre

Fact: Harris and Klebold violated close to 20 firearms laws in obtaining weapons. Would 21 laws really have made a difference? The two shotguns and one rifle used by Harris and Klebold were purchased by a girlfriend who passed a background check, and the TEC-9 handgun used was already banned.

Myth: Children should be kept away from guns for their own safety

Fact: 0% of children that get guns from their parents commit gun-related crimes while 21% of those that get them illegally do.[81]

Fact: Children that acquire firearms illegally are twice as likely to commit street crimes (24%) than are those given a firearm by their parents (14%).[82]

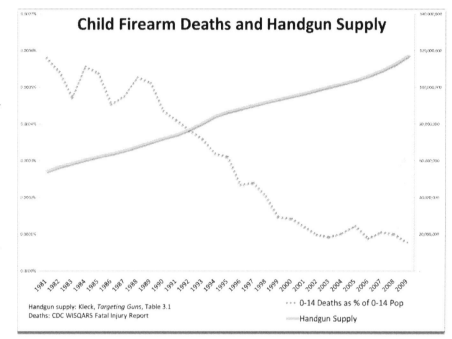

Child Firearm Deaths and Handgun Supply

Handgun supply: Kleck, *Targeting Guns*, Table 3.1
Deaths: CDC WISQARS Fatal Injury Report

· · · 0-14 Deaths as % of 0-14 Pop
——— Handgun Supply

Fact: Almost three times as many children (41%) consume illegal drugs if they also obtain firearms illegally, as compared to children given a firearm by their parents (13%).

Fact: In the 1950's, children routinely played cops and robbers, had toy guns, were given BB rifles and small caliber hunting rifles before puberty. Yet the homicide rate in the 1950's was almost half of that in the 1980's.[83]

Myth: More children are hurt with guns than by any other means

Fact: Barely more than 1% of <u>all unintentional deaths</u> for children in the U.S. between ages 0-14 are from firearms.[84]

---

[81] *Urban Delinquency and Substance Abuse* ,U.S. Justice Department, 2000

[82] Ibid

[83] *Vital Statistics* ,National Center for Health Statistics, , Revised July, 1999

[84] *Deaths: Final Data for 2006*, National Vital Statistics Reports, 2009, Center for Disease Control

Fact: The Center for Disease Control, a federal agency, disagrees. According to them, in 1998, children 0-14 years died from the following causes in the U.S. [85]

Fact: Children are 12 times more likely to die in an automobile accident than from gun-related homicides or legal interventions (being shot by a police officer, for example) if they are age 0-14. For the group 0-24 years old (which bends the definition of "child" quite a bit), the rate is still 8.6 times higher for cars.[86]

Cause	Deaths
Transportation	1,499
Suffication	1,118
Drowning	726
Fire	308
Natural	97
Poisioning	94
Firearm	62
Blunt force	60

Ages 0-14 - CDC WISQARS Fatal Injury Reports, 2010

Fact: In 2001, there were only 72 accidental firearm deaths for children under age 15, as opposed to over 2,100 children who drowned (29 times as many drowning deaths as firearm deaths).[87]

Fact: Accidental firearm injuries for children and adolescents dropped 37% from 1993 to 1997, with the fastest drop – a 64% reduction – being for children.[88]

Fact: Boys who own legal firearms have much lower rates of delinquency and drug use than non-owners of guns.[89]

Fact: The *non-gun* homicide rate of children in the U.S. is more than twice as high as in other western countries. And eight times as many children die from *non-gun* violent acts than from gun crimes.[90] This indicates that the problem is violence, not guns.

Fact: Fatal gun accidents for children ages 0-14 declined by almost 83% from 1981 to 2002[91] – all while the number of handguns per capita increased over 41%.[92]

Fact: 82% of homicides of children age 13 and under were committed *without* a gun.[93]

MYTH: IF IT SAVES THE LIFE OF ONE CHILD, IT IS WORTH IT

Fact: Firearms in private hands are used an estimated 2.5 million times (or 6,849 times each day) each year to prevent crime;[94] this includes rapes, aggravated assaults, and kidnapping.

---

[85] *Deaths: Final for 1998*,Center for Disease Control, vol. 48 no. 11., July 24, 2000

[86] *National Vital Statistics Report* , National Center for Health Statistics, 1997

[87] *20 Leading Causes of Unintentional Injury Deaths* ,Center for Disease Control, , United States, 2001, (All Races, Both Sexes, Ages: 1-14)

[88] *Firearms Injury Surveillance Study*, Centers for Disease Control and Prevention, December 2001

[89] *Urban Delinquency and Substance Abuse* ,U.S. Department of Justice, National Institute of Justice, Office of Juvenile Justice and Delinquency Prevention, NCJ-143454, , August 1995

[90] *Kids and Guns* ,Office of Juvenile Justice and Delinquency Prevention , "", 2000

[91] National Center for Health Statistics

[92] BATF estimates on handguns in circulation, BATF, Firearms Commerce in the United States 2001/2002

[93] FBI Uniform Crime Statistics, 1997

[94] Gary Kleck, Criminologist, Florida State University, 1997

The number of innocent children protected by firearm owning parents far outweighs the number of children harmed.

Fact: Most Americans (firearm owners or not) believe that the way parents raise kids is what causes gun violence (or just violence in general). Among <u>non-firearm</u> owners, 38% said it was parental neglect that causes youth violence, while only 28% thought it was due to the availability of guns.[95] They may be right, given that most homicides of children under age five are by their own parents. Of homicides among children ages 5 and younger: 31% were killed by their own mothers and another 31% were killed by their own fathers.[96]

---

[95] Gallup/Women.com poll, May 2000

[96] *FBI, Supplementary Homicide Reports*, 1976-98

ACCIDENTAL DEATHS

MYTH: ACCIDENTAL GUN FATALITIES ARE A SERIOUS PROBLEM

Fact: Firearm misuse causes only a small number of accidental deaths in the U.S.[97] For example, compared to being accidentally killed by a firearm, you are:

- Five times more likely to burn to death
- Five times more likely to drown
- 17 times more likely to be poisoned
- 17 times more likely to fall to your death
- And 68 times more likely to die in an automobile accident

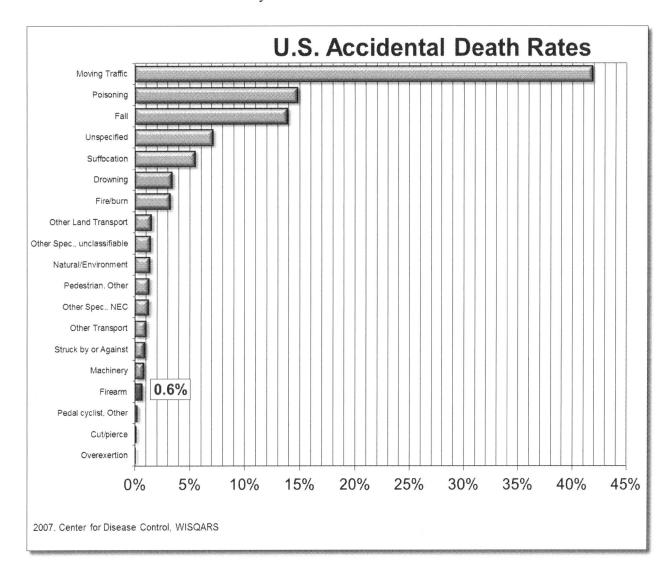

U.S. Accidental Death Rates

2007, Center for Disease Control, WISQARS

---

[97] *WISQARS Injury Mortality Report*, Center for Disease Control, 2007

Fact: In 2007, there were only 54 accidental gun deaths for children under age 13. About 12 times as many children died from drowning during the same period.[98]

Fact: In 2007, there were 999 drowning victims and 137 firearm-related accidental deaths in age groups 1 through 19. This despite the fact that firearms outnumber pools by a factor of more than 30:1. Thus, the risk of drowning in a pool is nearly 100 times higher than dying from a firearm-related accident for everyone, and nearly 500 times for children ages 0-5.[99]

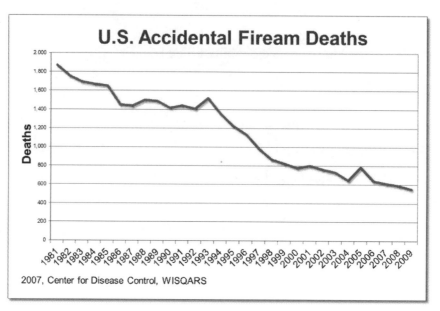

Fact: Medical mistakes kill 400,000 people per year – the equivalent of almost three fully loaded Boeing 747 jet crashes per day – or about 286 times the rate of all accidental firearm deaths.[100] This translates into 1 in 6 doctors causing an accidental death, and 1 in 56,666 gun owners doing the same.

Fact: Only 2% of gun deaths are from accidents, and some insurance investigations indicate that many of these may not be accidents after all.[101]

Fact: Around 2,000 patients each year – six per day – are accidentally killed or injured in hospitals by registered nurses.[102]

MYTH: HANDGUNS ARE UNSAFE AND CAUSE ACCIDENTS

Fact: Most fatal firearm accidents involve long guns, which are more deadly. These are typically hunting accidents.[103]

Fact: Handguns have triggers that are difficult for small (child) hands to operate, and are rarely the cause of accidents.[104]

---

[98] Ibid

[3] National Center for Health Statistics, and the National Spa and Pool Institute

[100] *Medical death statistics, Gun deaths*, Dr. David Lawrence, CEO Kaiser Permanente, CDC report 1993

[101] *Targeting Guns: Firearms and Their Control*, Gary Kleck, Aldine de Gruyter 1997 at 293-324

[102] Chicago Tribune report, Sept 10, 2000

[103] *Targeting Guns: Firearms and Their Control*, Gary Kleck , Aldine de Gruyter 1997, at 293-324

MYTH: INNOCENT BYSTANDERS ARE OFTEN KILLED BY GUNS

Fact: Less than 1% of all gun homicides involve innocent bystanders.[105]

MYTH: CITIZENS ARE TOO INCOMPETENT TO USE GUNS FOR PROTECTION

Fact: About 11% of police shootings kill an innocent person - about 2% of shootings by citizens kill an innocent person. The odds of a defensive gun user killing an innocent person are less than 1 in 26,000[106] despite American citizens using guns to prevent crimes almost 2,500,000 times every year.

Fact: Most firearm accidents are caused by people with various forms of poor self-control. These include alcoholics, people with previous criminal records, people with multiple driving accidents, and people who engage in other risky behaviors.[107]

MYTH: GUN ACCIDENTS ARE FLOODING EMERGENCY ROOMS

Fact: The rate of gun accidents is so low that the U.S. Consumer Product Safety Commission doesn't even mention them in their annual safety reports.

MYTH: "JUNK" GUNS ARE DANGEROUS AND SHOULD BE BANNED

Fact: In the history of the state of California, not one lawsuit against a gun maker had been filed (until 2003) based on a weapon being defective or poorly designed.[108]

MYTH: GUNS SHOULD BE MADE TO CONFORM TO PRODUCT LIABILITY LAWS

Fact: Guns are already covered under product liability laws. If you have a defective gun that does not operate properly, you can sue the gun maker.

---

[104] Ibid.

[105] *Stray bullets and 'mushrooms'*, Sherman, Steele, Laufersweiler, Hoffer and Julian, Journal of Quantitative Criminology, 1989

[106] *Shall Issue: The New Wave of Concealed Handgun Permit Laws,* C. Cramer, and D. Kopel, Independence Institute Issue Paper. October 17, 1994

[107] *Targeting Guns: Firearms and Their Control*, Gary Kleck, Aldine de Gruyter, 1997, at 307, 312

[108] California Trial Lawyers Association, 1998

Shooting The Bull

By Gun Facts author, Guy Smith

In politics, everyone lies. Voters distrust everything they are told by politicians, the media and even their neighbors. Despite universal suspicion of news and opinion makers, very few people understand how political lies are created and thus most folk are unable to dissect spin and discover truth. *Shooting the Bull* details how all political falsehoods are created, why they work and how to detect them.

Nowhere on the political landscape are more lies told than within the churning bowels of the gun control industry. Fighting America's revolutionary reluctance to submit and the public's continuing fear of criminals not currently incarcerated in Congress, voters have resisted legislative agendas proposed by The Brady Campaign, Violence Policy Center and the Clinton administration. For decades, significant victories have eluded their ilk, leaving only one strategy with which to sway voters – lying.

Shooting the Bull serves two purposes. First, it catalogs the common canards of politicians and activists. Readers will recognize how they have been psychologically scammed by special interests and deceived by elected sycophants. They will also experience disquieting revelations as they discover forms of fibs they had previously encountered but not recognized. By the end of the book, readers will be infinitely more cynical about politicians and propagandists and be equipped to dissect future electoral effluvium.

The second purpose of *Shooting the Bull* is to document the deceits peddled by the gun control lobby. Each chapter is devoted to at least one major initiative proffered by anti-gun activists, exposing their falsities through dissection of their motives, methods and inconvenient facts. The art and science of political pretense is illustrated through Senator Dianne Feinstein's "assault weapon" ban, the Million Mom March's campaign to register all guns and license all owners, and Michael Moore's deluded "documentaries"

Buy Today at Amazon.com

CONCEALED CARRY LAWS AND WEAPONS

MYTH: CONCEALED CARRY DOESN'T PREVENT CRIMES

Fact: News reports tell many stories of armed civilians preventing mass murder in public. A few selected at random include:

- A citizen with a gun stopped a knife-wielding man as he began stabbing people in a Salt Lake City store.
- Two men retrieved firearms from their cars and stopped a mass murder at the Appalachian School of Law.
- Citizen takes out shooter while police were pinned down in Early, Texas.
- Citizen stops apartment shoot-up in Oklahoma City.

MYTH: CONCEALED CARRY LAWS INCREASE CRIME

Fact: Thirty-nine states,[109] comprising the majority of the American population, are "right-to-carry" states. Statistics show that in these states the crime rate fell (or did not rise) after the right-to-carry law became active (as of July, 2006). Nine states restrict the right to carry and two deny it outright.

---

[109]At publication time two more states, Kansas and Nebraska, have passed shall-issue legislation, but insufficient data was available to determine how the change has impacted crime rates.

Fact: Crime rates involving gun owners with carry permits have consistently been about 0.02% of all carry permit holders since Florida's right-to-carry law started in 1988.[110]

Fact: After passing their concealed carry law, Florida's homicide rate fell from 36% above the national average to 4% below,[111] and remains below the national average (as of the last reporting period, 2005).

Fact: In Texas, murder rates fell 50% faster than the national average in the year after their concealed carry law passed. Rape rates fell 93% faster in the first year after enactment, and 500% faster in the second.[112] Assaults fell 250% faster in the second year.[113]

Fact: More to the point, crime is significantly higher in states without right-to-carry laws.[114]

Fact: States that disallow concealed carry have violent crime rates 11% higher than national averages.[115]

Fact: Deaths and injuries from mass public shootings fall dramatically after right-to-carry concealed handgun laws are enacted. Between 1977 and 1995,[116] the average death rate from mass shootings plummeted by up to 91% after such laws went into effect, and injuries dropped by over 80%.[117]

Type of Crime	% Higher in Restrictive States
Robbery	105%
Murder	86%
Assault	82%
Violent Crime	81%
Auto theft	60%
Rape	25%

---

[110] Florida Department of Justice, 1998

[111] *Shall issue: the new wave of concealed handgun permit laws,* Cramer C and Kopel D. Golden CO: Independence Institute Issue Paper. October 17, 1994

[112] Some criminologist believe measuring first year change is shortsighted as it takes more than a year for permits to be issued, reach critical quantities, and for the criminally minded to recognize the new situation and avoid violent confrontations.

[113] Bureau of Justice Statistics, online database, reviewing Texas and U.S. violent crime from 1995-2001.

[114] *Crime, Deterrence, and Right-to-Carry Concealed Handguns*, Lott, John R., and Mustard, David B. J. of Legal Studies, vol.26, n.1, pp.1-68 (Jan. 1997): This study involved county level crime statistics from *all* 3,054 counties in the U.S., from 1977 through 1992. During this time ten states adopted right-to-carry laws. It is estimated that if all states had adopted right-to-carry laws, in 1992 the US would have avoided 1,400 murders, 4,200 rapes, 12,000 robberies, 60,000 aggravated assaults – and saved over $5,000,000,000 in victim expenses.

[115] FBI, Uniform Crime Reports, 2004 - excludes Hawaii and Rhode Island - small populations and geographic isolation create other determinants to violent crime.

[116] Federal legislation created a national "gun-free schools" policy, effective in 1996. Some criminologists maintain this created a new dynamic, encouraging mass murder on campus. Thus after 1995 it is increasing difficult to make comparisons based on the effects of CCWs and mass shootings.

[117] *Multiple Victim Public Shootings, Bombings, and Right-to-Carry Concealed Handgun Laws: Contrasting Private and Public Law Enforcement*, John Lott and William Landes, Law School of the University of Chicago, Law & Economics Working Paper No. 73

MYTH: CONCEALED CARRY PERMIT HOLDERS SHOOT POLICE

Fact: The Violence Police Center started listing instances of CCW holders shooting police.[118] From May 2007 through November 2009 (2.5 years) they recorded nine police deaths, three in one mass killing by a white supremacist using an AK-47 rifle. Of the nine, five have yet to have a trial or conviction.

MYTH: PEOPLE WITH CONCEALED WEAPONS PERMITS WILL COMMIT CRIMES

Fact: The results for the first 30 states that passed "shall-issue" laws for concealed carry permits are similar.

Fact: In Texas, citizens with concealed carry permits are 14 times less likely to commit a crime. They are also five times less likely to commit a violent crime.[128]

State[119]	Permits issued	Revoked permits	% Re-voked	Violent Crime Rate Change[120]
Florida	1,327,321[121]	4,129	0.3%	-30.5%
Virginia	50,000[122]	0	0.0%	-21.9%
Arizona	63,000[123]	50	0.9%	-28.7%
North Carolina	59,597[124]	1,274	1.2%	-26.4%
Minnesota	46,636[125]	12	0.03%	8.0%[126]
Michigan	155,000[127]	2,178	0.1%	1.4%

Fact: People with concealed carry permits are:[129]

- 5.7 times <u>less</u> likely to be arrested for violent offenses than the general public
- 13.5 times <u>less</u> likely to be arrested for non-violent offenses than the general public

---

[118] *Law Enforcement Officers Killed by Concealed Handgun Permit Holders*, VPC, December 13, 2009

[119] Reports were as received. No selection or filtering process was used.

[120] Violent crime rates are from inception of "shall issue" CCW through 2006, the most recent period available through the Bureau of Justice Statistics online database.

[121] October 1987 through Jan 2008

[122] 1995 – no follow-up data available

[123] 1994 through 2007

[124] 1995 through 2004

[125] 2002 through 2006

[126] In 2005 and 2006, Minnesota had an abnormal spike in robbery and aggravated assaults. The first three years of CCW in Minnesota saw violent crime rates being roughly stable and the problem has somewhat abated since then.

[127] 2001 through 2007

[128] Texas Department of Public Safety and the U.S. Census Bureau, reported in San Antonio Express-News, September, 2000

[129] *An Analysis of the Arrest Rate of Texas Concealed Carry Handgun License Holders as Compared to the Arrest Rate of the Entire Texas Population*, William E. Sturdevant, PE, September 11, 1999

Fact: Even gun control organizations agree it is a non-problem, as in Texas – "because there haven't been Wild West shootouts in the streets".[130]

Fact: Of 14,000 CCW licensees in Oregon, only 4 (0.03%) were convicted of the criminal (not necessarily violent) use or possession of a firearm.

Fact: "I'm detecting that I'm eating a lot of crow on this issue ... I think that says something, that we've gotten to this point in the year and in the third largest city in America there has not been a single charge against anyone that had anything to do with a concealed handgun."[131]

Fact: In Florida, a state that has allowed concealed carry since late 1987, you are twice as likely to be attacked by an <u>alligator</u> as by a person with a concealed carry permit.[132]

MYTH: CONCEALED GUNS IN BARS WILL CAUSE VIOLENCE

Fact: In Virginia, in the first year where CCW holders were allowed to, the number of major crimes involving firearms at bars and restaurants statewide declined 5.2% The crimes that occurred during the law's first year were relatively minor.[133]

MYTH: TEXAS CCW HOLDERS ARE ARRESTED 66% MORE OFTEN

Fact: Most arrests cited are not any form of violent crime (includes bounced checks or tax delinquency).[134]

Fact: The Violence Policy Center "study" only includes arrests, not <u>convictions</u>.

Fact: Many of these arrests in this premature VPC "study" came in the early years of Texas CCWs when the law was not understood by most of the law enforcement community or prosecutors.

Fact: Compared to the entire

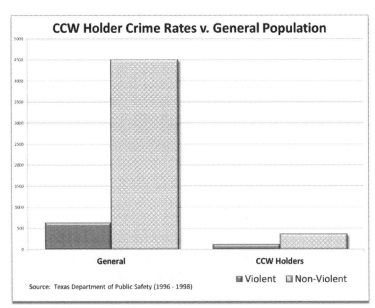

---

[130] Nina Butts, Texans Against Gun Violence, Dallas Morning News, August 10, 2000

[131] John Holmes, Harris County [Houston, TX] District Attorney, *In Session: Handgun Law's First Year Belies Fears of 'Blood in the Streets,"* Texas Lawyer, December 9, 1996

[132] *Concealed Weapons/Firearms License Statistical Report*, Florida Department of State, 1998 – Florida Game and Fresh Water Fish Commission, December 1998

[133] *Gun Crimes Drop at Virginia Bars And Restaurants*, Richmond Times-Dispatch, August 14, 2011, reporting data from the Virginia State Police

[134] *Basis For Revocation Or Suspension Of Texas Concealed*, Texas Department of Public Safety, December 1, 1998

---

population, Texas CCW holders are about 7.6 times <u>less</u> likely to be arrested for a <u>violent</u> crime.[135] The numbers breakdown as follows:

- 214,000 CCW holders[136]
- 526 (0.2%) felony arrests of CCW holders that have been adjudicated
- 100 (0.05%) felony convictions

Fact: A different study concludes that the four year violent crime arrest rate for CCW holders is 128 per 100,000. For the general population, it is 710 per 100,000. In other words, CCW holders are 5.5 times <u>less</u> likely to commit a violent crime.[137]

Fact: "I lobbied against the law in 1993 and 1995 because I thought it would lead to wholesale armed conflict. That hasn't happened. All the horror stories I thought would come to pass didn't happen. No bogeyman. I think it's worked out well, and that says good things about the citizens who have permits. I'm a convert."[138]

Fact: "It has impressed me how remarkably responsible the permit holders have been."[139]

MYTH: CCWs WILL LEAD TO MASS PUBLIC SHOOTINGS

Fact: Multiple victim public shootings drop in states that pass shall-issue CCW legislation.[140]

Fact: CCW holders have prevented or curtailed mass public shootings – Pearl, Mississippi (Pearl Junior High School), Edinboro, Pennsylvania (Parker Middle School), Winnemucca, Nevada (Players Bar and Grill), Colorado Springs, Colorado (New Life Church).

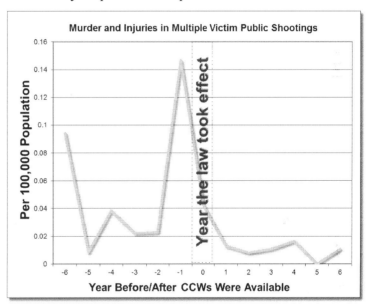

---

[135] Texas Department of Corrections data, 1996-2000, compiled by the Texas State Rifle Association, www.tsra.com/arrests.htm

[136] These are year 2000 records. As of 2005, the number of Texas concealed carry permit holders was 248,874.

[137] *An Analysis Of The Arrest Rate Of Texas Concealed Handgun License Holders As Compared To The Arrest Rate Of The Entire Texas Population*, William E. Sturdevant, PE, September 11, 1999

[138] Glenn White, President of the Dallas Police Association, Dallas Morning News, December 23, 1997

[139] Colonel James Wilson, Director Texas Department of Public Safety, Dallas Morning News, Jun 11, 1996

[140] *Multiple Victim Public Shootings, Bombings, and Right-to-Carry Concealed Handgun Laws: Contrasting Private and Public Law Enforcement*, Lott John R., Landes William M.; University of Chicago – covers years 1977 to 1995

Myth: People do not need concealable weapons

Fact: In 80% of gun defenses, the defender used a concealable handgun. A quarter of the gun defenses occurred in places away from the defender's home.[141]

Fact: 77% of all violent crime occurs in public places.[142] This makes concealed carry necessary for almost all self-defense needs. But due to onerous laws forbidding concealed carry, only 26.8% of defensive gun uses occurred away from home.[143]

Fact: Often, small weapons that are capable of being concealed are the only ones usable by people of small stature or with physical disabilities.

Fact: The average citizen doesn't <u>need</u> a Sport Utility Vehicle, but driving one is arguably safer than driving other vehicles. Similarly, carrying a concealable gun makes the owner – and his or her community – safer by providing protection not otherwise available.

Myth: Police and prosecutors are against concealed carrying by citizens

Fact: 66% of police chiefs believe that citizens carrying concealed firearms reduce rates of violent crime.[144]

Fact: "All the horror stories I thought would come to pass didn't happen ...I think it's worked out well, and that says good things about the citizens who have permits. I'm a convert."[145]

Fact: "I ... [felt] that such legislation present[ed] a clear and present danger to law-abiding citizens by placing more handguns on our streets. Boy was I wrong. Our experience in Harris County, and indeed statewide, has proven my fears absolutely groundless".[146]

Fact: "Virginia has not turned into Dodge City. We have not seen a problem."[147]

Fact: "The concerns I had – with more guns on the street, folks may be more apt to square off against one another with weapons – we haven't experienced that."[148]

Fact: "… to the best of my knowledge, we have not had an issue. I had expected there would be a lot more problems … But it has actually worked out."[149]

---

[141] *Armed Resistance to Crime: The Prevalence and Nature of Self-Defense with a Gun*, by Gary Kleck and Marc Gertz, in The Journal of Criminal Law & Criminology, Northwestern University School of Law, Volume 86, Number 1, Fall, 1995

[142] *Criminal Victimization in the United States*, U.S. Bureau of Justice Statistics, 1993

[143] Kleck and Gertz, National Self Defense Survey, 1995

[144] National Association of Chiefs of Police, 17th Annual National Survey of Police Chiefs & Sheriffs, 2005

[145] Glenn White, president, Dallas Police Association, Dallas Morning News, December 23, 1997

[146] John B. Holmes, Harris County Texas district attorney, Dallas Morning News, December 23, 1997

[147] Jerry Kilgore, Virginia Public Safety Secretary, Fredricksburg Freelance Star, February 2, 1996

[148] Chief Dennis Nowicki, Charlotte-Mecklenburg North Carolina Police, News and Observer, November 24, 1997

[149] Lt. William Burgess of the Calhoun County (Michigan) Sheriff Department, Battle Creek Enquirer, January 28, 2005

Fact: Explain this to the <u>Law Enforcement Alliance of America</u>, <u>Second Amendment Police Department</u>, and Law Enforcement for the Preservation of the Second Amendment, all of whom support shall-issue concealed carry laws.

CRIME AND GUNS

Basic to the debates on gun control is the fact that most violent crime is committed by repeat offenders. Dealing with recidivism is key to solving violence.

- 71% of gunshot victims had previous arrest records.

- 64% had been convicted of a crime.

- Each had an average of 11 prior arrests.[150,151]

- 63% of *victims* have criminal histories and 73% of the time they know their assailant (twice as often as victims without criminal histories).[152]

Most gun violence is between criminals. This should be the public policy focus.

MYTH: GUNS ARE NOT A GOOD DETERRENT TO CRIME

Fact: Guns prevent an estimated 2.5 million crimes a year or 6,849 every day.[153] Often the gun is never fired and no blood (including the criminal's) is shed.

Fact: Property crime rates are dropping (especially burglaries). The chart shows the legal handgun supply in America (mainly in civilian hands) to the property crime rate.[154]

Fact: Every day 400,000 life-threatening violent crimes are prevented using firearms.

Fact: 60% of convicted felons admitted that they avoided committing crimes when they knew the victim was armed. 40% of convicted felons admitted that they avoided committing crimes when they thought the victim might be armed.[155]

SOURCE: Crime data from Bureau of Justice Statistics online.

---

[150] Richard Lumb, Paul Friday, City of Charlotte Gunshot Study, Department of Criminal Justice, 1994

[151] *Homicides and Non-Fatal Shootings: A Report on the First 6 Months Of 2009*, Milwaukee Homicide Review Commission, July 13, 2009

[152] *Firearm-related Injury Incidents in 1999 – Annual Report*, San Francisco Department of Public Health and San Francisco Injury Center, February 2002

[153] *Targeting Guns*, Dr. Gary Kleck, Criminologist, Florida State University, Aldine, 1997

[154] *National Crime Victimization Survey, 2000*, Bureau of Justice Statistics, BATF estimates on handgun supply

[155] *Armed and Considered Dangerous: A Survey of Felons and Their Firearms*, James Wright and Peter Rossi, Aldine, 1986

Fact: Felons report that they avoid entering houses where people are at home because they fear being shot.[156]

Fact: 59% of the burglaries in Britain, which has tough gun control laws, are "hot burglaries"[157] which are burglaries committed while the home is occupied by the owner/renter. By contrast, the U.S., with more lenient gun control laws, has a "hot burglary" rate of only 13%.[158]

Fact: Washington DC has essentially banned gun ownership since 1976[159] and has a murder rate of 56.9 per 100,000. Across the river in Arlington, Virginia, gun ownership is less restricted. There, the murder rate is just 1.6 per 100,000, less than three percent of the Washington, DC rate.[160]

Fact: 26% of all retail businesses report keeping a gun on the premises for crime control.[161]

Fact: In 1982, Kennesaw, GA passed a law requiring heads of households to keep at least one firearm in the house. The residential burglary rate dropped 89% the following year.[162]

Fact: A survey of felons revealed the following:[163]

- 74% of felons agreed that, "one reason burglars avoid houses when people are at home is that they fear being shot during the crime."

- 57% of felons polled agreed, "criminals are more worried about meeting an armed victim than they are about running into the police."

MYTH: PRIVATE GUNS ARE USED TO COMMIT VIOLENT CRIMES

Fact: 90% of all violent crimes in the U.S. do not involve firearms of any type.[164]

Fact: Even in crimes where the offender possessed a gun during the commission of the crime, 83% did not use or threaten to use the gun.[165]

Fact: Fewer than 1% of firearms will ever be used in the commission of a crime.[166]

---

[156] Ibid

[157] A "hot burglary" is when the burglar enters a home while the residents are there

[158] Dr. Gary Kleck, Criminologist, Florida State University (1997) and Kopel (1992 and 1999)

[159] The Supreme Court invalidated the D.C. handgun ban in the Heller case (2008), but the city has made obtaining a handgun very difficult via local legislation.

[160] *Crime in the United States*, FBI, 1998

[161] *Crime Against Small Business*, U.S. Small Business Administration, Senate Document No. 91-14, 1969

[162] *Crime Control Through the Private Use of Armed Force*, Dr. Gary Kleck, Social Problems, February 1988

[163] *The Armed Criminal in America: A Survey of Incarcerated Felons*, U.S. Bureau of Justice Statistics Federal Firearms Offenders study, 1997: National Institute of Justice, Research Report, July 1985, Department of Justice

[164] Bureau of Alcohol, Tobacco and Firearms, 1998

[165] National Crime Victimization Survey, 1994, Bureau of Justice Statistics

[166] FBI Uniform Crime Statistics, 1994

Fact: Two-thirds of the people who die each year from gunfire are criminals being shot by other criminals.[167]

Fact: 94.4% of gang murders are committed with guns.[168] Gangs are responsible for between 48% and 90% of all violent crimes.[169]

MYTH: HIGH CAPACITY, SEMI-AUTOMATICS ARE PREFERRED BY CRIMINALS

Fact: The use of semi-automatic handguns in crimes is slightly lower than the ratio of semi-automatic handguns owned by private citizens. Any increase in style and capacity simply reflects the overall supply of the various types of firearms.[170]

MYTH: BANNING "SATURDAY NIGHT SPECIALS" REDUCES CRIME

Fact: This was the conclusion of the Johns Hopkins University Center for Gun Policy and Research – and it is wrong. They studied firearm homicide rates from Maryland after passage of a Saturday Night Special ban in 1998. It seems the firearm homicide rate has not subsided and remained between 68-94% higher than the national average through 2008.[171]

Fact: Even banning guns does not slow down criminals. In the U.K., where private ownership of firearms is practically forbidden, criminals have and use guns regularly, and even build their own. One enterprising fellow converted 170 starter pistols to functioning firearms and sold them to gangs. Hundreds of such underground gun factories have been established, contributing to a 35% jump in gun violence.[172]

MYTH: CRIMINALS PREFER "SATURDAY NIGHT SPECIALS"[173]

Fact: "Saturday Night Specials" were used in less than 3% of crimes involving guns.[174]

Fact: Fewer than 2% of all "Saturday Night Specials" made are used in crimes.

Fact: "What was available was the overriding factor in weapon choice [by criminals]."[175]

MYTH: GUN SHOWS ARE SUPERMARKETS FOR CRIMINALS

Fact: Only 0.7% of convicts bought their firearms at gun shows. 39.2% obtained them from illegal street dealers.[176]

---

[167] Ibid

[168] *Homicide trends in the United States*, Bureau of Justice Statistics, January 17 2007

[169] *2011 National Gang Threat Assessment*, FBI, September 2011

[170] *Targeting Guns*, Dr. Gary Kleck, Criminologist, Florida State University, Aldine, 1997

[171] *Injury Mortality Reports 1999-2008*, Center for Disease Control, online database

[172] *Gun crime spreads 'like a cancer' across Britain*, The Guardian, Oct 5, 2003

[173] "Saturday Night Special" is a term, with racist origin, describing an inexpensive firearm. Part of the origin of the term came from "suicide special", describing an inexpensive handgun purchased specifically for committing suicide. The racist origins are too detestable to repeat here.

[174] FBI Uniform Crime Statistics, 1994

[175] *Violent Encounters: A Study of Felonious Assaults on Our Nation's Law Enforcement Officers*, U.S. Department of Justice, August 2006

Fact: Fewer than 1% of "crime guns" were obtained at gun shows.[177] This is a reduction from a 1997 study that found 2% of guns used in criminal offenses were purchased at gun shows.[178]

Fact: The FBI concluded in one study that no firearms acquired at gun shows were used to kill police officers. "In contrast to media myth, none of the firearms in the study were obtained from gun shows."[179]

Fact: Only 5% of metropolitan police departments believe gun shows are a problem.[180]

Fact: Only 3.5% of youthful offenders reported that they obtained their last handgun at a gun show.[181]

Fact: 93% of guns used in crimes are obtained illegally (i.e., not at gun stores or gun shows).[182]

Fact: At most, 14% of all firearms traced in investigations were purchased at gun shows.[183] But this includes all firearms that the police traced, whether or not they were used in crimes, which overstates the acquisition rate.

Fact: Gun dealers are federally licensed. They are bound to stringent rules for sales that apply equally whether they are selling firearms from a storefront or a gun show.[184]

Fact: Most crime guns are either bought off the street from illegal sources (39.2%) or through family members or friends (39.6%).[185]

MYTH: 25-50% OF THE VENDORS AT MOST GUN SHOWS ARE "UNLICENSED DEALERS"

Fact: There is no such thing as an "unlicensed dealer," except for people who buy and sell antique – curio – firearms as a hobby (not a business).

Fact: This 25-50% figure can only be achieved if you include those dealers *not selling guns* at these shows. These non-gun dealers include knife makers, ammunition dealers, accessories dealers, military artifact traders, clothing vendors, bumper sticker sellers, and hobbyists. In short, *50% of the vendors at shows are not selling firearms at all!*

---

[176] *Firearm Use by Offenders*, Bureau of Justice Statistics, February 2002

[177] Ibid

[178] *Homicide in Eight U.S. Cities*, National Institute of Justice, December 1997

[179] *Violent Encounters: A Study of Felonious Assaults on Our Nation's Law Enforcement Officers*, U.S. Department of Justice, August 2006

[180] *On the Front Line: Making Gun Interdiction Work*, Center to Prevent Handgun Violence, February 1998, survey of 37 police departments in large cities

[181] *Patterns in Gun Acquisition and Use by Youthful Offenders in Michigan*, Timothy S. Bynum, Todd G. Beitzel, Tracy A. O'Connell & Sean P. Varano, 1999

[182] BATF, 1999

[183] BATF, June 2000, covers only July 1996 through December 1998

[184] BATF, 2000

[185] *Firearm use by Offenders*, Bureau of Justice Statistics, November 2001

Myth: Regulation of gun shows would reduce "straw sales"

Fact: The main study that makes this claim had no scientific means for determining what sales at the show were "straw sales." Behaviors that Dr. Wintemute cited as "clear evidence" of a straw purchase were observational only and were more likely instances of more experienced acquaintances helping in a purchase decision. No attempts were made to verify that the sales in question were straw sales.[186]

Myth: Prison isn't the answer to crime control

Fact: From 1960-1980, per capita imprisonment for violent crimes fell from 738 to 227. In the same period, violent crime rates nationwide tripled.

Fact: Why does crime rise when criminals are released from prison early? Because they are likely to commit more crimes. 67.5% were re-arrested for new felonies or serious misdemeanors within three years. Extrapolating, those released felons killed another 2,282 people.[187]

Fact: 45% of state prisoners were, at the time they committed their offense, under conditional supervision in the community – either on probation or on parole.[188] Keeping violent convicts in prison would reduce violent crimes.

Fact: Homicide convicts serve a little more than ½ of their original sentences.[189] Given that men tend to be less prone to violent behavior as they age[190], holding them for their full sentences would probably reduce violence significantly.

Fact: Los Angeles County saw repeat offender and re-arrest rates soar after authorities closed jails and released prisoners early. In less than three years, early release of prisoners in LA resulted in:[191]

- 15,775 rearrested convicts
- 1,443 assault charges[192]
- 518 robbery charges[42]
- 215 sex offense charges[42]
- 16 murder charges[42]

Fact: In 1991, 13,200 homicides were committed by felons on parole or probation. For comparison sake, this is about ½ of the 1999 annual gun death totals (keep in mind that gun deaths fell from 1991 to 1999).

---

[186] *Gun shows across a multistate American gun market*, Dr. GJ Wintemute, British Medical Journal, 2007

[187] *Reentry Trends in the U.S., Recidivism*, Department of Justice, 1999

[188] US Bureau of Justice Statistics, 1991

[189] *Firearm Use by Offenders*, Bureau of Justice Statistics, November , 2001

[190] Homicide rates peak in the 18-24 year old group, Bureau of Justice Statistics, online database

[191] *Releasing Inmates Early Has a Costly Human Toll*, Los Angeles Times, May 14, 2006

[192] Keep in mind these are just charges. Each arrested convict may have committed multiple crimes.

Myth: Waiting periods prevent rash crimes and reduce violent crime rates

Fact: The "time-to-crime" of a firearm ranges from one to 12 years making it rare that a newly purchased firearm is used in a crime.[193]

Fact: The national five-day waiting period under the Brady Bill had no impact on murder or robbery. In fact, there was a slight increase in rape and aggravated assault, indicating no effective suppression of certain violent crimes. Thus, for two crime categories, a possible effect was to delay law-abiding citizens from getting a gun for protection. The risks were greatest for crimes against women.[194]

Fact: Comparing homicide rates in 18 states that had waiting periods and background checks before the Brady Bill with rates in the 32 states that had no comparable laws, the difference in change of homicide rates was "insignificant".[195]

Myth: Gun makers are selling plastic guns that slip through metal detectors

Fact: There is no such thing as a 'plastic gun'. This myth started in 1980[196] when Glock began marketing a handgun with a polymer frame, not the entire firearm. Most of a Glock is metal (83% by weight) and detectable in common metal and x-ray detectors. "[D]espite a relatively common impression to the contrary, there is no current non-metal firearm not reasonably detectable by present technology and methods in use at our airports today, nor to my knowledge, is anyone on the threshold of developing such a firearm."[197]

Incidentally, Glock is one of the favorite handguns of police departments *because it is lightweight, thanks to the polymer frame.*

Myth: Machine guns[198] are favored by criminals

Fact: In the drug-ridden Miami of 1980, less than 1% of all gun homicides were with machine guns.[199]

Fact: None of over 2,220 firearms recovered from crime scenes by the Minneapolis police in 1987-89 were machine guns.[200]

Fact: 0.7% of seized guns in Detroit in 1991-92 were machine guns.[201]

---

[193] Bureau of Alcohol, Tobacco and Firearms as reported by Time Magazine, July 12, 2002

[194] Dr. John Lott Jr., University of Chicago School of Law, 1997

[195] Dr. Jens Ludwig , Dr. Philip J. Cook, Journal of the American Medical Association, August 2000

[196] Heckler and Koch made a polymer framed firearm earlier, in 1968, but the myth seems to have erupted after Glock began promoting theirs to police departments.

[197] Billie Vincent, FAA Director of Civil Aviation Security, House Subcommittee on Crime, May 15, 1986

[198] In this myth, "machine gun" represents "fully automatic" firearms, ones that fire bullets as long as the trigger is pulled.

[199] Miami Herald, August 23, 1984, based on figures from Dr. Joseph Davis, Dade County medical examiner

[200] 1994, Minnesota Medical Association Firearm Injury Prevention Task Force

GUNS AND CRIME PREVENTION

MYTH: PRIVATE OWNERSHIP OF GUNS IS NOT EFFECTIVE IN PREVENTING CRIME

Fact: Every year, people in the United States use guns to defend themselves against criminals an estimated 2,500,000 times – more than 6,500 people a day, or once every 13 seconds.[202] Of these instances, 15.7% of the people using firearms defensively stated that they "almost certainly" saved their lives by doing so.

Firearms are used <u>60 times</u> more often to protect lives than to take lives.

Fact: The number of times per year an American uses a firearm to deter a home invasion alone is 498,000.[203]

Fact: In 83.5% (2,087,500) of these successful gun defenses, the attacker either threatened or used force first, proving that guns are very well suited for self-defense.

Fact: The rate of defensive gun use (DGU) is six times that of criminal gun use.[204]

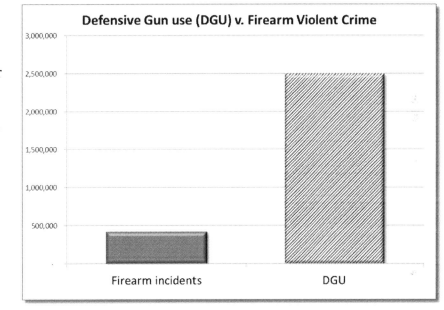

Fact: Of the 2,500,000 times citizens use guns to defend themselves, 92% merely brandish their gun or fire a warning shot to scare off their attackers.

Fact: Less than 8% of the time does a citizen wound his or her attacker, and in less than one in a thousand instances is the attacker killed.[205]

Fact: In one local review of firearm homicide, more than 12% were civilian legal defensive homicides.[206]

---

[201] J. Gayle Mericle, 1989, Unpublished report of the Metropolitan Area Narcotics Squad, Will and Grundy Counties

[202] *Journal of Criminal Law and Criminology*, Kleck and Gertz, Fall 1995

[203] *Estimating intruder-related firearm retrievals in U.S. households, 1994.* Robin M. Ikeda , *Violence and Victims*, Winter 1997

[204] Crime statistics: Bureau of Justice Statistics - *National Crime Victimization Survey* (2005). DGU statistics: *Targeting Guns*, Kleck (average of 15 major surveys where DGUs were reported)

[205] *Targeting Guns*, Kleck, from the National Self-Defense Survey, 1995

Fact: For every accidental death (802), suicide (16,869) or homicide (11,348)[207] with a firearm (29,019), 13 lives (390,000)[208] are preserved through defensive use.

Fact: When using guns in self-defense, 91.1% of the time, not a single shot is fired.[209]

Fact: After the implementation of Canada's 1977 gun controls prohibiting handgun possession for protection, the "breaking and entering" crime rate rose 25%, surpassing the American rate.[210]

MYTH: ONLY POLICE SHOULD HAVE GUNS

Fact: "Most criminals are more worried about meeting an armed victim than they are about running into the police."[211]

Fact: 11% of police shootings kill an innocent person - about 2% of shootings by citizens kill an innocent person.[212]

Fact: Police have trouble keeping their own guns. Hundreds of firearms are missing from the FBI and 449 of them have been involved in crimes.[213]

Fact: People who saw the helplessness of the L.A. Police Department during the 1992 King Riots or the looting and violence in New Orleans after hurricane Katrina know that citizens need guns to defend themselves.

Fact: "In actual shootings, citizens do far better than law enforcement on hit potential. They hit their targets and they don't hit other people. I wish I could say the same for cops. We train more, they do better."[214]

MYTH: YOU ARE MORE LIKELY TO BE INJURED OR KILLED USING A GUN FOR SELF-DEFENSE

Fact: You are far more likely to <u>survive</u> violent assault if you defend yourself with a gun.[215]

---

[206] *Death by Gun: One Year Later*, Time Magazine, May 14, 1990

[207] *Unintentional Firearm Deaths, 2001*, U.S. Centers for Disease Control and Prevention, National Center for Injury Prevention and Control

[208] *Targeting Guns*, Gary Kleck, Aldine de Gruyter, 1997

[209] *National Crime Victimization Survey*, 2000

[210] *Residential Burglary: A Comparison of the United States, Canada and England and Wales*, Pat Mayhew, National Institute of Justice., Wash., D.C., 1987

[211] *Armed and Considered Dangerous: A Survey of Felons and Their Firearms*, Wright and Rossi, 1986

[212] *Shall issue: the new wave of concealed handgun permit laws*, Clayton Cramer, David Kopel, Independence Institute Issue Paper. October 17, 1994

[213] ABC News, July 17, 2001

[214] Sheriff Greg White, Cole County, Missouri, *Guns to be allowed on campus?*, KRCG News, July 31, 2009

[215] *The Value of Civilian Handgun Possession as a Deterrent to Crime or a Defense Against Crime*, Don B. Kates, 1991 American Journal of Criminal Law

---

MYTH: GUNS ARE NOT EFFECTIVE IN PREVENTING CRIME AGAINST WOMEN

Fact: Of the 2,500,000 annual self-defense cases using guns, more than 7.7% (192,500) are by women defending themselves against sexual abuse.

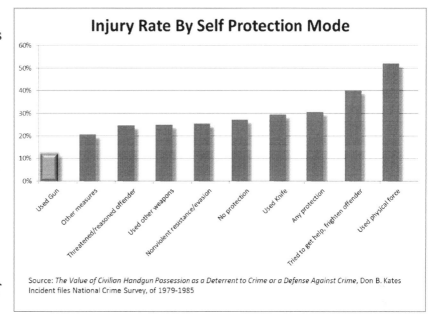

Source: *The Value of Civilian Handgun Possession as a Deterrent to Crime or a Defense Against Crime*, Don B. Kates Incident files National Crime Survey, of 1979-1985

Fact: When a woman was armed with a gun or knife, only 3% of rape attacks were completed, compared to 32% when the woman was unarmed.[216]

Fact: The probability of serious injury from an attack is 2.5 times greater for women offering no resistance than for women resisting with guns. Men also benefit from using guns, but the benefits are smaller: Men are 1.4 times more likely to receive a serious injury.[217]

Fact: 28.5% of women have one or more guns in the house.[218]

Fact: 41.7% of women either own or have convenient access to guns.[219]

Fact: In 1966, the city of Orlando responded to a wave of sexual assaults by offering firearms training classes to women. Rapes dropped by nearly 90% the following year.

Reported Rape Rates 1995–2003 (per 100,000 pop.)			
	1995	2003	% Change
Australia	72.5	91.7	+26.5
United Kingdom	43.3	69.2	+59.8
United States	37.1	32.1	-13.5

Fact: Firearm availability appears to be particularly useful in avoiding rape. The United Kingdom virtually banned handgun ownership. During the same period handgun ownership in the United States steadily rose. Yet the rate of rape decreased in the United States and skyrocketed in the other countries, as shown in the table.

Fact: More Americans believe having a gun in the home makes them safer. This belief grows every year the survey is taken.[220]

---

[216] *Law Enforcement Assistance Administration, Rape Victimization in 26 American Cities*, U.S. Department of Justice, 1979

[217] *National Crime Victimization Survey*, Department of Justice

[218] *2001 National Gun Policy Survey of the National Opinion Research Center: Research Findings*, Smith, T, National Opinion Research Center, University of Chicago, December 2001.

[219] Ibid

[220] *Americans by Slight Margin Say Gun in the Home Makes It Safer*, Gallup Poll, October 20, 2006

Fact: Arthur Kellerman, a researcher whose work is often cited by gun control groups, said "If you've got to resist, your chances of being hurt are less the more lethal your weapon. If that were my wife, would I want her to have a .38 Special in her hand? Yeah."[221]

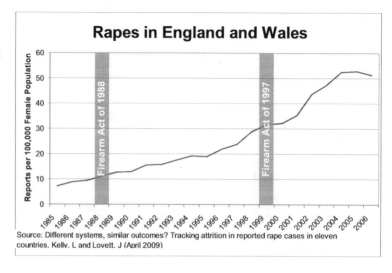

Rapes in England and Wales

Source: Different systems, similar outcomes? Tracking attrition in reported rape cases in eleven countries. Kelly. L and Lovett. J (April 2009)

---

[221] *Gun Crazy*, S.F. Examiner, April 3, 1994

GOVERNMENT, GUN LAWS, AND SOCIAL COSTS

MYTH: GUN CONTROL REDUCES CRIME

Fact: There are more than 22,000[222] gun laws at the city, county, state, and federal level. If gun control worked, then we should be free of crime. Yet the U.S. government "found insufficient evidence to determine the effectiveness of any of the firearms laws or combinations of laws reviewed on violent outcomes" [223] and also concluded in one study that none of the attackers interviewed was "hindered by any law – federal, state or local –that has ever been established to prevent gun ownership. They just laughed at gun laws."[224]

Fact: Violent crime appears to be encouraged by gun control. Most gun control laws in the United States have been written since 1968, yet the murder rate rose during the 70s, 80s and early 90s.[225]

Fact: In 1976, Washington, D.C. enacted one of the most restrictive gun control laws in the nation. The city's murder rate rose 134 percent through 1996 while the national murder rate has dropped 2 percent.[226]

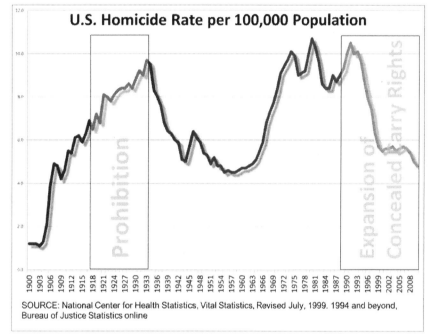

SOURCE: National Center for Health Statistics, Vital Statistics, Revised July, 1999. 1994 and beyond, Bureau of Justice Statistics online

Fact: Among the 15 states with the highest homicide rates, 10 have restrictive or very restrictive gun laws.[227]

Fact: Maryland claims to have the toughest gun control laws in the nation and ranks #1 in robberies and #4 in both violent crime and murder.[228] The robbery rate is 70% more than the

---

[222] *Under the Gun: Weapons, Crime, and Violence in America*, Bureau of Alcohol, Tobacco and Firearms estimate and reported via James Wright, Peter H. Rossi, Kathleen Daly, 1983

[223] *First Reports Evaluating the Effectiveness of Strategies for Preventing Violence: Firearms Laws*, CDC, Task Force on Community Preventive Services, Oct 3, 2003 – a systematic review of 51 studies that evaluated the effects of selected firearms laws on violence

[224] *Violent Encounters: A Study of Felonious Assaults on Our Nation's Law Enforcement Officers*, U.S. Department of Justice, August 2006

[225] National Center for Health Statistics, Vital Statistics, Revised July, 1999

[226] Dr. Gary Kleck, University of Florida using FBI Uniform Crime Statistics, 1997

[227] Ibid

national average.[229] These numbers are likely low because one of their more violent cities, Baltimore, failed to report their crime levels.

Fact: In 2000, 20% of U.S. homicides occurred in four cities with just six percent of the population – New York, Chicago, Detroit, and Washington, D.C. – most of which had a virtual prohibition on privately owned handguns at the time.[230]

Fact: The landmark federal Gun Control Act of 1968, banning most interstate gun sales, had no discernible impact on the criminal acquisition of guns from other states.[231]

Fact: Washington, D.C.'s 1976 ban on the ownership of handguns (except those already registered in the District) was not linked to any reduction in gun crime in the nation's capital.[232]

Fact: New York has one of the most restrictive gun laws in the nation – and 20% of the armed robberies.[233]

Fact: In analyzing 10 different possible reasons for the decline in violent crime during the 1990s, gun control was calculated to have contributed nothing (high imprisonment rates, more police and legalized abortion were considered the primary factors, contributing as much as 28% of the overall reduction).[234]

MYTH: GUNS SHOULD BE REGISTERED AND LICENSED LIKE CARS

Fact: You do not need a license to buy a car. You can buy as many as you want and drive them all you like on your own property without a license.

Fact: Cars are registered because they are (a) sources of tax revenue, (b) objects of fraud in some transactions, and (c) significant theft targets. Thus we ask the government to track them.

Fact: There is no constitutionally guaranteed right to keep and bear automobiles, and thus they are subject to greater regulation than guns.

Fact: There are more guns in the U.S. than cars (228,000,000 guns and 207,754,000 automobiles). Yet you are 31 times more likely to be accidentally killed by a car than a gun according to the National Safety Council[235] ... despite cars having been registered and licensed for almost 100 years.

---

[228] *Index of Crime by State*, FBI Uniform Crime Reports (UCR) for 2000, p. 79, Table 5

[229] FBI Uniform Crime Reports, September 15, 2000

[230] Ibid

[231] *Under the Gun*, Wright, Rossi, Daly, University of Massachusetts, 1981

[232] Ibid

[233] Ibid

[234] *Understanding Why Crime Fell in the 1990s*, Steven Levit, Journal of Economic Perspectives, Winter 2004

[235] Automobiles estimates: Federal Highway Administration, October 1998. Firearm estimates: FBI Uniform Crime Statistics, 1996.

Myth: The Brady Bill caused a decrease in gun homicides

Fact: All violent crime (including gun and non-gun murders) fell during the same period, 1992 to 1997. However, the percent of homicides committed with guns stayed the same. In 1992, 68% of murders were committed with guns; in 1997, it was still 68%.[236] Thus, the decreased gun homicide rate was part of an overall declining crime rate, not an effect of the Brady Bill.

Fact: Gun possession by criminals has risen in the post-Brady years – 18% of state prisoners (was 16% before Brady) and 15% of federal prisoners (was 12% before Brady) were caught with firearms.[237]

Fact: The Brady Bill is not enforced. In 2006, of 77,000 Field Office referrals for instant background check violations (25,259 of which NICS identified as buyers with felony records), 0.4% (273) were ever charged with a crime and 0.1% (73) were convicted.[238]

Fact: The Brady Bill has so far failed to appreciably save lives.[239]

Fact: Violent crime started falling in 1991, three years before passage of the Brady Bill. The Brady Bill did not apply in 18 states, yet violent crime in those states fell just as quickly.[240]

Fact: A majority of Americans agree that the bill is worthless. 51% believe the act has been ineffective at reducing violent crime, and 56% believe it has had no impact on reducing the number of homicides in the U.S.[241]

Myth: Gun laws are being enforced

Fact: During the Clinton administration, federal prosecutions of gun-related crimes dropped more than 44 percent.[242]

Fact: Of the 3,353 prohibited individuals that obtained firearms, the Clinton administration only investigated 110 of them (3.3%).[243]

Fact: Despite 536,000 prohibited buyers caught by the National Instant (Criminal Background) Check System (NICS), only 6,700 people (1.25%) have been charged for these firearms violations. This includes 71% of the violations coming from convicted or indicted

---

[236] FBI Uniform Crime Reports for 1992 and 1997

[237] *Firearm Use by Offenders*, Bureau of Justice Statistics, November 2001

[238] *Enforcement of the Brady Act, 2006*, Regional Justice Information Service, study funded by Bureau of Justice Statistics, Office of Justice Programs, U.S. Department of Justice.

[239] Dr. Jens Ludwig, Dr. Philip J. Cook, Journal of the American Medical Association, August 2000

[240] *Gun Licensing Leads to Increased Crime, Lost Lives*, Prof. John Lott, L.A. Times, Aug 23, 2000, based on both the FBI Uniform Crime Statistics for 1990s and the U.S. Justice Department Crime Victimization Survey

[241] Portrait of America survey, August 2000

[242] Transactional Records Access Clearinghouse (TRAC) at Syracuse University covering 1992 through 1998

[243] General Accounting Office (GAO) 2000 audit of the National Instant Check System between 11/30/98 and 11/30/99. This stat needs to be tempered by the fact that many initial rejections were due to database errors – false positives – where the buyer was later approved.

felons.[244] None of these crimes were prosecuted by the Federal government in 1996, 1997, or 1998.[245]

Fact: In 1998, the government prosecuted just eight children for gun law violations.[246] In that same year, there were only:

- 8 prosecutions for juvenile handgun possession.
- 6 prosecutions for handgun transfer to juveniles.
- 1 prosecution for Brady Bill violations.

Fact: Some of the reasons listed for not prosecuting known gun criminals include "minimal federal interest" and "DOJ/U.S. Attorney policy".[247]

Fact: Half of referrals concerning violent criminals were closed without investigation or prosecution.[248]

Fact: The average sentence for a federal firearms violation dropped from 57 months to 46 months from 1996 to 1998.[249]

Fact: 18-20 year olds commit over 23% of all gun murders.[250] None of these criminals are allowed by law to purchase a handgun, but the Federal government under Clinton rarely enforced this law.[251]

Fact: Project Exile in Richmond, Virginia prosecutes felons caught with guns, and prosecutes them using Federal laws that require mandatory imprisonment. The first year result was a 33% drop in homicides for the Richmond Metro area in a year where the national murder rate was climbing.[252] This shows that enforcement works. And according to Andrew McBride of the Richmond Justice Department Office, these cases are as easy to prosecute as "picking change up off the street."

---

[244] Bureau of Justice Statistics, Federal Firearm Offenders and Background Checks for Firearm Transfers, June 4, 2000

[245] U.S. Justice Department statistics, 1999

[246] Ibid

[247] Bureau of Justice Statistics, Federal Firearm Offenders and Background Checks for Firearm Transfers, June 4, 2000

[248] General Accounting Office report on the Implementation of NICS, February, 2000

[249] Ibid

[250] United States Treasury and Justice Department Report, 1999

[251] *Federal Firearm Offenders* report, Bureau of Justice Statistics, June 4, 2000 – firearm suspects declined for prosecution by U.S. attorneys ... some of the reasons listed for not prosecuting known gun criminals include "minimal federal interest" and "DOJ/U.S. Attorney policy"

[252] FBI Uniform Crime Statistics, 1999

MYTH: FEDERAL GUN CRIME PROSECUTIONS INCREASED 25%

Fact: 1992: 9,885 BATF referrals for federal firearm purchase violations
1998: 4,391 (a 56% drop)
1999: 5,489 (a fictitious "25% increase")[253]

Fact: 1992: 12,084 BATF referrals for all firearm law violations
1998: 5,620 (a 53% drop)

MYTH: THE SOCIAL COST OF GUN VIOLENCE IS ENORMOUS

Fact: Because guns are used an estimated 2.5 million times per year to *prevent* crimes, the cost savings in personal losses, police work, and court and prison expenses vastly outweighs the cost of criminal gun violence and gun accidents. The net savings, under a worst-case scenario, is about $3.5 billion a year.[254]

Fact: Guns are used 65 times more often to prevent a crime than to commit one.[255]

Fact: The medical cost of gun violence is only 0.16% of America's annual health care expenditures.[256]

Fact: Drunken drivers killed 15,935 people in 1998[257] while homicides with guns were 12,102 for the same year. Drunken drivers continue to kill people randomly despite a decade of increased strictness and social pressure against drunk drivers.

MYTH: THE SOCIAL COST OF GUN VIOLENCE IS $20-100 BILLION

Fact: One "study"[258] included the lifetime earnings of people that die from guns, not just the true social costs. This included lost incomes of criminals killed by law-abiding citizens, costs associated with suicides, the "emotional costs experienced by relatives and friends of gunshot victims, and the fear and general reduction in quality of life ... including people who are not victimized". If the same methodology were used to calculate the social savings from private gun ownership, we would see a benefit to society of half a trillion dollars, or 10% of the 1999 US Gross Domestic Product.

Fact: Another "study"[259] started by polling people how much they would be willing to have their taxes raised in order to reduce firearm violence by 30%, and then projected these bids to the entire U.S. population. This seriously flawed methodology does not measure the "cost" of the problem, just what people are willing to spend to reduce the problem.

---

[253] BATF, 1999

[254] *Suing Gun Manufacturers: Hazardous to Our Health*, Sterling Burnett, National Center for Policy Analysis, 1999

[255] Taking Dr. Gary Kleck's estimate of 2.5 million gun defenses each year, divided by the FBI estimates of crimes committed with a firearm.

[256] *Shooting in the dark: estimating the cost of firearm injuries*, Max W and Rice DP, Health Affairs, 1993

[257] Compiled by Mothers Against Drunk Driving (MADD)

[258] *The Financial Costs of Gun Violence*, Linda Gunderson, Annals of Internal Medicine, September 21, 1999

[259] *Gun Violence : The Real Costs*, Ludwig, Cook, 2000

Fact: Social saving from private ownership is not used in these studies. One study[260] indicated between 240,000 and 300,000 defensive uses of firearms, as described by the victim, "… almost certainly had saved a life."

Myth: Gun "buy back" programs get guns off the streets

Fact: According to the federal government, gun 'buybacks' have "no effect".[261]

Fact: "Buy backs" remove no more than 2% of the firearms within a community. And the firearms that are removed do not resemble guns used in crimes. *"There has never been any effect on crime results seen".*[262]

Fact: Up to 62% of people trading in a firearm still have another at home, and 27% said they would or might buy another within a year.[263]

Fact: More than 50% of the weapons bought via a gun buy back program were over 15 years old, whereas almost half of firearms seized from juveniles are less than three years old.[264]

Fact: According to a variety of sources, the actual effect is that gun buy back programs:

- Disarm future crime victims, creating new social costs
- Give criminals an easy way to dispose of evidence
- Are turned in by those least likely to commit crimes (the elderly, women, etc.)
- Results in cheap guns being bought and sold to the government for a profit
- Cause guns to be stolen and sold to the police, creating more crime
- Seldom return stolen guns to their rightful owners

Fact: "They do very little good. Guns arriving at buy backs are simply not the same guns that would otherwise have been used in crime. If you look at the people who are turning in firearms, they are consistently the least crime-prone [ed: least likely to commit crimes]: older people and women."[265]

Myth: Closing down "kitchen table" gun dealers will reduce guns on the street

Fact: 43% of gun dealers had no inventory and sold no guns at all. Congressional testimony documented that the large number of low-volume gun dealers is a direct result of BATF policy. The BATF once prosecuted gun collectors who sold as few as three guns per year at gun shows, claiming that they were unlicensed, and therefore illegal, gun dealers. To avoid such harassment, thousands of American gun collectors became licensed gun dealers. Now the BATF claims not to have the resources to audit the paperwork monster it created.

---

[260] *Armed Resistance To Crime*, Kleck, Gertz, Journal of Criminal Law and Criminology, vol. 86, no. 1, 1995: 150

[261] *Preventing Crime: What Works, What Doesn't, What's Promising*, National Institute of Justice, July 1998

[262] Garen Wintemute, Violence Prevention Research Program, U.C., Davis, 1997

[263] Jon Vernick, John Hopkins Center for Gun Policy and Research, Sacramento and St. Louis studies

[264] District of Columbia buyback program, 1999

[265] David Kennedy, Senior Researcher, Harvard University Kennedy School Program in Criminal Justice, in appearance on Fox News, November 22, 2000

Fact: Reforms of the Federal Firearm Licensing program – mainly focused at small volume retailers and traders – produced no significant results in firearm crime rates.[266]

MYTH: ONLY THE GOVERNMENT SHOULD HAVE GUNS

Fact: Only if you want criminals to have them as well. Loose inventory controls are notorious in government agencies, as shown by the Immigration and Naturalization Service (INS) that has "misplaced" 539 weapons, including a gas-grenade launcher and 39 automatic rifles or machine guns. Six guns were eventually linked to crimes (two guns had been used in armed robberies, one confiscated in a raid on a drug laboratory and two others during arrests. One was being held as evidence in a homicide investigation).[267] And in July of 2001, it was reported that the FBI lost 449 weapons, including machine guns.

MYTH: "SAFE STORAGE" LAWS PROTECT PEOPLE

Fact: 15 states that passed "safe storage" laws saw 300 more murders, 3,860 more rapes, 24,650 more robberies, and over 25,000 more aggravated assaults in the first five years. On average, the annual costs borne by victims averaged over $2.6 billion as a result of lost productivity, out-of-pocket expenses, medical bills, and property losses. "The problem is, you see no decrease in either juvenile accidental gun deaths or suicides when such laws are enacted, but you do see an increase in crime rates." [268]

Fact: Only five American children under the age of 10 died of accidents involving handguns in 1997.[269] Thus, the need for "safe storage" laws appears to be low.

Fact: In Merced California, an intruder stabbed three children to death with a pitchfork. The oldest child had been trained by her father in firearms use, but could not save her siblings from the attacker because the gun was locked away to comply with the state's "safe storage" law.[270]

MYTH: LOCAL BACKGROUND CHECKS REDUCE GUN SUICIDES[271]

Fact: The research reports only a change in the "firearm suicide rate" and not the total suicide rate. No strict correlation between overall suicides and background checks exists.

Fact: The report did not explain the disparity between states that all had local background checks and radically different suicide rates (Hawaii with 2.82/100,000 and Washington with 9.28/100,000). Nor did it explain how states with different levels of background checks have

---

[266] Christopher Koper of Pennsylvania's Jerry Lee Center of Criminology, reported in Criminology & Public Policy, American Society of Criminology, March 2002

[267] Associated Press report, April 17, 2001

[268] *Safe Storage Gun Laws: Accidental Deaths, Suicides, and Crime*, Prof. John Lott, Yale School of Law, March 2000

[269] Ibid

[270] Sierra Times and various wire services, September, 2000

[271] This myth derives from *Firearm Death Rates and Association with Level of Firearm Purchase Background Check*, Steven A. Sumner, Layde, Guse, American Journal of Preventive Medicine, Volume 35, Issue 1, Pages 1-86 (July 2008)

---

nearly identical suicide rates (Hawaii has local checks and a 2.82 firearm suicide rate while New York uses state checks and has a lower 2.72 rate).

Fact: The report was a two year snapshot, which makes trending impossible. Proper analysis would have examined change in suicide rates in states before and after background check policy changed.

Fact: Researchers split homicide and suicide propensity controls by age (65+ for suicides and 15-29 for homicides).

POLICE AND GUNS

MYTH: POLICE FAVOR GUN CONTROL

Fact: 94% of law enforcement officials believe that citizens should be able to purchase firearms for self-defense and sporting purposes.[272]

Fact: 65.8% believe there should be no gun rationing, such as 'one gun per month' schemes.

Fact: 97.9% of police officers believe criminals are able to obtain any type of firearm through illegal means.

Fact: "Gun control has not worked in D.C. The only people who have guns are criminals. We have the strictest gun laws in the nation and one of the highest murder rates. It's quicker to pull your Smith & Wesson than to dial 911 if you're being robbed."[273]

MYTH: POLICE ARE OUR PROTECTION - PEOPLE DON'T NEED GUNS

Fact: Tell that to 18,209 murder victims, 497,950 robbery victims, and 96,122 rape victims that the police could not help.[274]

Fact: The courts have consistently ruled that the police do not have an obligation to protect individuals. In Warren v. District of Columbia Metropolitan Police Department, 444 A.2d 1 (D.C. App. 1981), the court stated: `... courts have without exception concluded that when a municipality or other governmental entity undertakes to furnish police services, it assumes a duty only to the public at large and not to individual members of the community.' Well, except for politicians whom receive taxpayer-financed bodyguards.

Fact: There are not enough police to protect everyone. In 1999, there were about 150,000 police officers on duty at any one time.[275]

- This is <u>on-duty</u> police. This includes desk clerks, command sergeants, etc. – far fewer than 150,000 cops are cruising your neighborhood.
- There were approximately 271,933,702 people living in the United States in 1999.[276]
- Thus *there is only one on-duty cop for every 1,813 citizens!*

Fact: Former Florida Attorney General Jim Smith told Florida legislators that police responded to only 200,000 of 700,000 calls for help to Dade County authorities.

Fact: The United States Department of Justice found that, in 1989, there were 168,881 crimes of violence for which police had not responded within 1 hour.

Fact: 95% of the time police arrive too late to prevent a crime or arrest the suspect.[277]

---

[272] *17th Annual National Survey of Police Chiefs & Sheriffs*, National Association of Chiefs of Police, 2005

[273] Lt. Lowell Duckett, Special Assistant to DC Police Chief; President, Black Police Caucus, The Washington Post, March 22, 1996

[274] 1997 FBI Uniform Crime Statistics

[275] US Justice Department, 1998

[276] US Census Bureau, 1999 estimate

Fact: In over 90% of U.S. cities, technology does not give police dispatchers the location of a cellular telephone caller[278], making police protection nearly impossible for travelers.

Fact: 75% of protective/restraining orders are violated and police often won't enforce them unless they witness the violation. [279]

Fact: Despite prompt law enforcement responses, most armed and violent attacks at schools were stopped by means other than law enforcement intervention.[280] Often these interventions were by administrators, teachers, or other students who were licensed to carry firearms.

MYTH: THE SUPPLY OF GUNS IS A DANGER TO LAW ENFORCEMENT

Fact: The courts kill cops by letting felons out of prison early. Of police killed in the line of duty:

- 70% are killed by criminals with prior arrest records
- 53% of these criminals have prior convictions
- 22% are on probation when the officer is killed

MYTH: "COP KILLER" BULLETS NEED TO BE BANNED

Fact: KTW rounds, wrongly labeled as "cop killer" bullets, were designed by police officers[281], for use by police to penetrate hard targets like car windshields. KTWs have never been sold to the general public.[282]

MYTH: TEFLON BULLETS ARE DESIGNED TO PENETRATE POLICE BULLET-PROOF VESTS

Fact: KTW rounds are Teflon coated to prevent heat build-up in a police officer's gun barrel, not to pierce body armor.[283]

---

[277] *This is 911 ... please hold,* Witkin, Gordon, Guttman, Monika and Lenzy, Tracy. U.S. News & World Report, June 17, 1998

[278] *911 - hello? Hellooooo?,* Susan Bahr, America's Network 103, April 1, 1999

[279] *Anti-stalking laws usually are unable to protect targets,* Ellen Sorokin, Washington Times, April 16, 2000

[280] *Threat Assessment In Schools*, U.S. Secret Service and U.S. Department of Education, 2002

[281] Developed by Daniel Turcos (a police sergeant) and Donald Ward (Dr. Kopsch's special investigator)

[282] *Cop Killer Bullets,* Mike Casey, July 2000

[283] Ibid

BALLISTIC "FINGERPRINTING"

MYTH: EVERY FIREARM LEAVES A UNIQUE "FINGERPRINT" THAT CAN PINPOINT THE FIREARM USED

Fact: A group of National Research Council scientists concluded that this has not yet been fully demonstrated. Their research suggests that the current technology for collecting and comparing images may not reliably distinguish very fine differences.[284]

Fact: "Firearms that generate markings on cartridge casings can change with use and can also be readily altered by the users. They are not permanently defined like fingerprints or DNA."[285]

Fact: "Automated computer matching systems do not provide conclusive results."[286]

Fact: "Because bullets are severely damaged on impact, they can only be examined manually".[287]

Fact: "Not all firearms generate markings on cartridge casings that can be identified back to the firearm."[288]

Fact: The same gun will produce different markings on bullets and casings, and different guns can produce similar markings.[289] Additionally, the type of ammunition actually used in a crime could differ from the type used when the gun was originally test-fired -- a difference that could lead to significant error in suggesting possible matches.[290]

Fact: The rifle used in the Martin Luther King assassination was test fired 18 times under court supervision, and the results showed that no two bullets were marked alike.[291] "Every test bullet was different because it was going over plating created by the previous bullet."

Fact: "The common layman seems to believe that two bullets fired from the same weapon are identical, down to the very last striation placed on them by the weapon. The trained firearms examiner knows how far that is from reality."[292]

---

[284] *Ballistic Imaging*, Daniel Cork, John Rolph, Eugene Meieran, Carol Petrie, National Research Council, 2008.

[285] *Feasibility of a Ballistics Imaging Database for All New Handgun Sales*, Frederic Tulleners, California Department of Justice, Bureau of Forensic Services, October, 2001 (henceforth *FBID*).

[286] Ibid.

[287] Ibid.

[288] Ibid.

[289] *Handbook of Firearms & Ballistics: Examining and Interpreting Forensic Evidence*, Heard, 1997.

[290] *Ballistic Imaging*, Daniel Cork, John Rolph, Eugene Meieran, Carol Petrie, National Research Council, 2008.

[291] *Ballistics 'fingerprinting' not foolproof*, Baltimore Sun, October 15, 2002.

[292] *AFTE Journal* , George G. Krivosta, Winter 2006 edition, Suffolk County Crime Laboratory, Hauppauge, New York.

MYTH: A DATABASE OF BALLISTIC PROFILES WILL ALLOW POLICE TO TRACE GUN CRIMES

Fact: The National Research Council deemed a national ballistics database as impractical due to practical limitations of current technology for generating and comparing images of ballistic markings.[293]

Fact: Maryland's ballistics database "is not doing anything"[294] and "has not met the mission statement of the state police."[295] In the first five years of implementation, it failed to lead to any criminal arrest or convictions, despite collecting over 80,000 specimens at a cost of $2,567,633.[296]

Fact: More than 70% of armed career criminals get their guns from "off-the-street sales" and "criminal acts" such as burglaries[297], and 71% of these firearms are stolen.[298] Tracing these firearms will not lead to the criminals, as the trail stops at the last legal owner.

Fact: Computer image matching of cartridges fails between 38-62% of the time, depending on whether the cartridges are from the same or different manufacturers.[299]

Fact: "Automated computer matching systems do not provide conclusive results" requiring that "potential candidates be manually reviewed".[300]

Fact: Criminals currently remove serial numbers from stolen guns to hide their origin. The same simple shop tools can change a ballistic profile within minutes. "The minor alteration required less than 5 minutes of labor".[301] Criminals will make changing ballistic profiles part of their standard procedures.

MYTH: BALLISTIC IMAGING IS USED IN MARYLAND AND NEW YORK AND SOLVES MANY CRIMES

Fact: Not so far. New York has not reported a single prosecution based on matched casings or bullets[302, 303, 304] and Maryland had only a single instance in 2005.[305] The cost for this lack of success in Maryland exceeds $2,500,000 a year, and in New York it exceeds $4,000,000.

---

[293] *Ballistic Imaging*, Daniel Cork, John Rolph, Eugene Meieran, Carol Petrie, National Research Council, 2008.

[294] *Maryland State Police Report Recommends Suspending Ballistics ID System*, Col. Thomas E. Hutchins, the state police superintendent, WBAL-TV web site, January 17, 2005.

[295] Sgt. Thornnie Rouse, Maryland State police spokesman, Ibid.

[296] *MD-IBIS Progress Report #2*, Maryland State Police Forensic Sciences Division, September 2004.

[297] *Protecting America*, Bureau of Alcohol, Tobacco and Firearms, 1992.

[298] *Armed and Considered Dangerous*, U.S. Department of Justice, 1986.

[299] *Feasibility of a Ballistics Imaging Database for All New Handgun Sales*, Frederic Tulleners, California Department of Justice, Bureau of Forensic Services, October, 2001.

[300] Ibid.

[301] Ibid.

[302] *NY ballistic database firing blanks?*, Associated Press, June 3, 2004.

[303] *Ballistics 'fingerprinting' not foolproof*, Baltimore Sun, October 15, 2002.

Fact: In Syracuse, the police have submitted fewer than 400 handguns for ballistic testing over a three-year span because the system is inefficient.[306]

MYTH: A BALLISTIC DATABASE IS INEXPENSIVE TO CREATE/MAINTAIN

Fact: " ... a huge inventory [of possible matches] will be generated for <u>manual review</u>." "[The] number of candidate cases will be so large as to be impractical and will likely create logistic complications so great that they cannot be effectively addressed".[307]

MYTH: POLICE WANT A BALLISTIC DATABASE

Fact: "The National Fraternal Order of Police does not support any Federal requirement to register privately owned firearms with the Federal government," the group said. "And, even if such a database is limited to firearms manufactured in the future, the cost to create and maintain such a system, with such small chances that it would be used to solve a firearm crime, suggests to the F.O.P. that these are law enforcement dollars best spent elsewhere."[308]

Fact: "We in law enforcement know it will not, does not, cannot work. Then, no one has considered the hundreds of millions of guns in the US that have never been registered or tested or printed."[309]

Fact: "One, the barrel is one of the most easily changed parts of many guns and two, the barrel, and the signature it leaves on a bullet, is constantly changing."[310]

---

[304] *Townsend backs New Rule on Sale of Assault Rifles*, Washington Post, October 30, 2002.

[305] *Ballistics Database Yields 1st Conviction*, Washington Post, April 2, 2005

[306] *400 guns wait to be traced by Syracuse police*, The Post-Standard, December 8, 2002.

[307] *Ballistics 'fingerprinting' not foolproof*, Baltimore Sun, October 15, 2002.

[308] *F.O.P. Viewpoint: Ballistics Imaging and Comparison Technology*, FOP Grand Lodge, October 2002.

[309] Joe Horn, Detective, Retired, Los Angeles County Sheriff's Dept., Small Arms Expert.

[310] Ted Deeds, chief operating officer of The Law Enforcement Alliance of America, Dodge Globe, Oct 24, 2002.

Shooting The Bull

By Gun Facts author, Guy Smith

In politics, everyone lies. Voters distrust everything they are told by politicians, the media and even their neighbors. Despite universal suspicion of news and opinion makers, very few people understand how political lies are created and thus most folk are unable to dissect spin and discover truth. *Shooting the Bull* details how all political falsehoods are created, why they work and how to detect them.

Nowhere on the political landscape are more lies told than within the churning bowels of the gun control industry. Fighting America's revolutionary reluctance to submit and the public's continuing fear of criminals not currently incarcerated in Congress, voters have resisted legislative agendas proposed by The Brady Campaign, Violence Policy Center and the Clinton administration. For decades, significant victories have eluded their ilk, leaving only one strategy with which to sway voters – lying.

Shooting the Bull serves two purposes. First, it catalogs the common canards of politicians and activists. Readers will recognize how they have been psychologically scammed by special interests and deceived by elected sycophants. They will also experience disquieting revelations as they discover forms of fibs they had previously encountered but not recognized. By the end of the book, readers will be infinitely more cynical about politicians and propagandists and be equipped to dissect future electoral effluvium.

The second purpose of *Shooting the Bull* is to document the deceits peddled by the gun control lobby. Each chapter is devoted to at least one major initiative proffered by anti-gun activists, exposing their falsities through dissection of their motives, methods and inconvenient facts. The art and science of political pretense is illustrated through Senator Dianne Feinstein's "assault weapon" ban, the Million Mom March's campaign to register all guns and license all owners, and Michael Moore's deluded "documentaries"

Buy Today at Amazon.com

GUNS IN OTHER COUNTRIES

MYTH: COUNTRIES WITH STRICT GUN CONTROL HAVE LESS CRIME

Fact: In America, we can demonstrate that private ownership of guns reduces crime, but from country to country there is no correlation between gun availability and the violent crime rate. Consider this:

Or, to use detailed data, we can contrast the per capita homicide rate with the per capita gun ownership rate between different industrialized countries (see graph below). Contrasting the data shows zero correlation between the availability of guns and the overall homicide rate.

		Crime Rate	
		High	**Low**
Gun Availability	**High**	United States	Switzerland
	Low	Mexico	Japan

Fact: Countries with the strictest gun-control laws also tended to have the highest homicide rates.[311]

Fact: According to the U.N., as of 2005, Scotland was the most violent country in the developed world, with people three times more likely to be assaulted than in America. Violent crime there has doubled over the last 20 years. 3% of Scots had been victims of assault compared with 1.2% in America.[312]

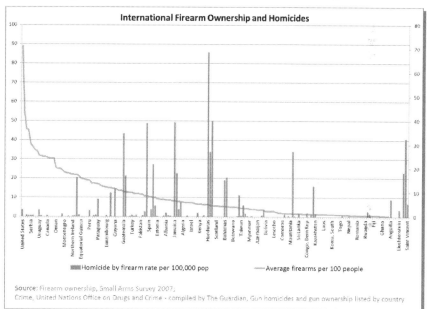

International Firearm Ownership and Homicides

Homicide by firearm rate per 100,000 pop — Average firearms per 100 people

Source: Firearm ownership, Small Arms Survey 2007; Crime, United Nations Office on Drugs and Crime - compiled by The Guardian, Gun homicides and gun ownership listed by country

Fact: "... the major surveys completed in the past 20 years or more provides no evidence of any relationship between the total number of legally held firearms in society and the rate of armed crime. Nor is there a relationship between the severity of controls imposed in various countries or the mass of bureaucracy involved with many control systems with the apparent ease of access to firearms by criminals and terrorists."[313]

---

[311] *Violence, Guns and Drugs: A Cross-Country Analysis*, Jeffery A. Miron, Department of Economics, Boston University, University of Chicago Press Journal of Law & Economics, October 2001.

[312] *Scotland tops list of world's most violent countries*, The Times, September 19, 2005

[313] *Minutes of Evidence*, Colin Greenwood, Select Committee on Northern Ireland Affairs, January 29, 2003.

Fact: Even if we examine just firearm ownership and firearm homicide by country, we see no correlation between the two.[314]

Fact: Switzerland has relatively lenient gun control for Europe[315], and has the third-lowest homicide rate of the top nine major European countries, and the same per capita rate as England and Wales.[316]

Fact: Indeed, the Swiss basically have a military rifle in nearly every closest. "Everybody who

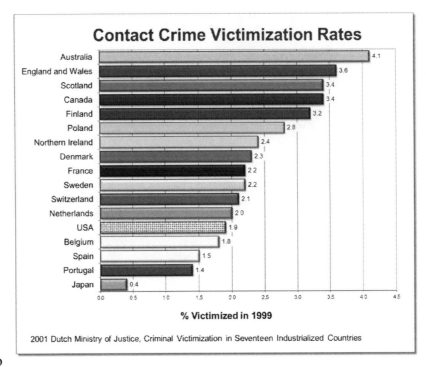

has served in the army is allowed to keep their personal weapon, even after the end of their military service."[317]

Fact: "We don't have as many guns [in Brazil] as the United States, but we use them more."[318] Brazil has mandatory licensing, registration, and maximum personal ownership quotas. It now bans any new sales to private citizens. Their homicide rate is almost three (3) times higher than the U.S.[319]

Fact: In Canada around 1920, before there was any form of gun control, their homicide rate was 7% of the U.S rate. By 1986, and after significant gun control legislation, Canada's homicide rate was 35% of the U.S. rate – a significant increase. [320] In 2003, Canada had a

---

[314] Source: Firearm ownership, Small Arms Survey 2007; Crime, United Nations Office on Drugs and Crime - compiled by The Guardian, *Gun homicides and gun ownership listed by country*

[315] In Switzerland, handguns are obtainable once a person obtains a simple police permit which is valid for six months. *Federal law over weapons, weapon accessories and ammunition (weapon law, WG)*, Federal Assembly of the Swiss Confederation, May 2007 - http://www.admin.ch/ch/d/sr/5/514.54.de.pdf

[316] Carol Kalish, International Crime Rates, Bureau of Justice Statistics Special Report (Washington: Department of Justice, May 1988). 1984 data for Switzerland, and the 1983 data for England and Wales.

[317] *Army rifles remain racked at home*, Swiss Defense Ministry statement, May 15, 2004, http://www.swissinfo.org .

[318] *Chocolates for guns? Brazil targets gun violence*, Rubem César Fernandes, executive secretary of Viva Rio, a nongovernmental agency that studies urban crime, Christian Science Monitor, August 10, 1999

[319] *Homicide trends in the United States*, U.S. data: Bureau of Justice Statistics, September, 2004. Brazil data: Nations Educational, Scientific and Cultural Organization, 2005.

[320] *Targeting Guns*, Gary Kleck, Aldine Transaction, 1997, at 360.

---

violent crime rate more than double that of the U.S. (963 vs. 475 per 100,000).[321]

Fact: Many of the countries with the strictest gun control have the highest rates of violent crime. Australia and England, which have virtually banned gun ownership, have the highest rates of robbery, sexual assault, and assault with force of the top 17 industrialized countries.[322]

Fact: The crime rate is 66% higher in four Canadian Prairie Provinces than in the northern US states across the border.[323]

Fact: Strict controls over existing arms failed in Finland. Despite needs-based licensing, storage laws and transportation restrictions,[324] Finland experienced a multiple killing school shooting in 2007.[325]

MYTH: BRITAIN HAS STRICT GUN CONTROL AND A LOW CRIME RATE

Fact: Since gun banning has escalated in the UK, the rate of crime – especially violent crime – has risen.

Fact: Ironically, firearm use in crimes in the UK has **doubled** in the decade since handguns were banned.[326]

Fact: Britain has the highest rate of violent

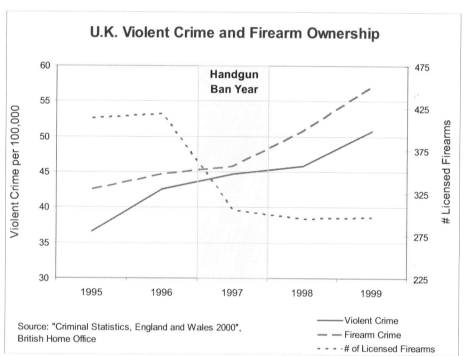

U.K. Violent Crime and Firearm Ownership

Source: "Criminal Statistics, England and Wales 2000", British Home Office

———— Violent Crime
— — — Firearm Crime
- - - - # of Licensed Firearms

---

[321] Juristat: Crime Statistics in Canada, 2004 and FBI Uniform Crime Statistics online.

[322] *Criminal Victimization in Seventeen Industrialized Countries*, Dutch Ministry of Justice, 2001.

[323] *A Comparison of Violent and Firearm Crime Rates in the Canadian Prairie Provinces and Four U.S. Border States, 1961-2003*, Parliamentary Research Branch of the Library of Parliament, March 7, 2005.

[324] *National Report by Finland*, United Nations Office for Disarmament Affairs.

[325] Pekka-Eric Auvinen shooting in Tuusula, Finland on November 8, 2007.

[326] *Weapons sell for just £50 as suspects and victims grow ever younger*, The Times, August 24, 2007.

---

crime in Europe, more so than the United States or even South Africa. They also have the second highest overall crime rate in the European Union. In 2008, Britain had a violent crime rate nearly five times higher than the United States (2034 vs. 446 per 100,000 population).[327]

Fact: 67% of British residents surveyed believed that "As a result of gun and knife crime [rising], the area I live in is not as safe as it was five years ago."[328]

Fact: U.K. street robberies soared 28% in 2001. Violent crime was up 11%, murders up 4%, and rapes were up 14%.[329]

Fact: This trend continued in the U.K. in 2004 with a 10% increase in street crime, 8% increase in muggings, and a 22% increase in robberies.

Fact: In 1919, before they had any gun control, the U.K. had a homicide rate that was 8% of the U.S. rate. By 1986, and after enacting significant gun control, the rate was 9% – practically unchanged.[330]

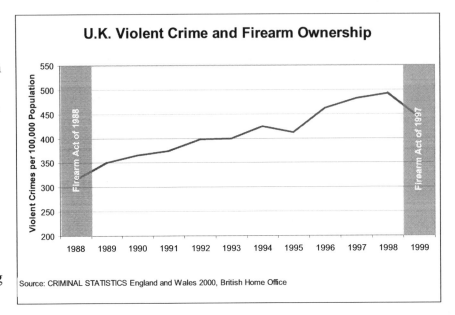

Source: CRIMINAL STATISTICS England and Wales 2000, British Home Office

Fact: "... [There is] nothing in the statistics for England and Wales to suggest that either the stricter controls on handguns prior to 1997 or the ban imposed since have controlled access to such firearms by criminals."[331]

Fact: Comparing crime rates between America and Britain is fundamentally flawed. In America, a gun crime is recorded as a gun crime. In Britain, a crime is only recorded when there is a final disposition (a conviction). All unsolved gun crimes in Britain are not reported as gun crimes, grossly undercounting the amount of gun crime there.[332] To make matters worse, British law enforcement has been exposed for falsifying criminal reports to create falsely lower crime figures, in part to preserve tourism.[333]

---

[327] *The most violent country in Europe: Britain is also worse than South Africa and U.S.*, Daily Mail, July 3, 2009, citing a joint report of the European Commission and United Nations.

[328] YouGov survey of 2,156 residents in Sept 2007.

[329] British Home Office, reported by BBC news, July 12, 2002.

[330] *Targeting Guns*, Gary Kleck, Aldine Transaction, 1997, at 359.

[331] *Minutes of Evidence*, Colin Greenwood, Select Committee on Northern Ireland Affairs, January 29, 2003.

[332] *Fear in Britain*, Gallant, Hills, Kopel, Independence Institute, July 18, 2000.

[333] *Crime Figures a Sham, Say Police*, Daily Telegraph, April 1, 1996.

Fact: An ongoing parliamentary inquiry in Britain into the growing number of black market weapons has concluded that there are more than three million illegally held firearms in circulation – double the number believed to have been held 10 years ago – and that criminals are more willing than ever to use them. One in three criminals under the age of 25 possesses or has access to a firearm. [334]

Fact: Handgun homicides in England and Wales reached an all-time high in 2000, years after a virtual ban on private handgun ownership. More than 3,000 crimes involving handguns were recorded in 1999-2000, including 42 homicides, 310 cases of attempted murder, 2,561 robberies and 204 burglaries. [335]

British Offenses in 2000	
Offense category	**Increase from pre-ban**
Armed robbery	170.1%
Kidnapping/abduction	144.0%
Assault	130.9%
Attempted murder	117.6%
Sexual assault	112.6%

Fact: Handguns were used in 3,685 British offenses in 2000 compared with 2,648 in 1997, an increase of 40%. [336] It is interesting to note:

- Of the 20 areas with the lowest number of legal firearms, 10 had an above average level of "gun crime."

- Of the 20 areas with the *highest* levels of legal guns, only 2 had armed crime levels above the average.

Fact: Between 1997 and 1999, there were 429 murders in London, the highest two-year figure for more than 10 years – nearly two-thirds of those involved firearms – in a country that has virtually banned private firearm ownership. [337]

Fact: Over the last century, the British crime rate was largely unchanged. In the late nineteenth century, the per capita homicide rate in Britain was between 1.0 and 1.5 per 100,000. [338] In the late twentieth century, after a near ban on gun ownership, the homicide rate is around 1.4. [339] This implies that the homicide rate did not vary with either the level of gun control or gun availability.

Fact: The U.K. has strict gun control and a rising homicide rate of 1.4 per 100,000. Switzerland has the highest per capita firearm ownership rate on the planet (all males age 20 to 42 are required to keep rifles or pistols at home) and has a homicide rate of 1.2 per 100,000. To date, there has never been a schoolyard massacre in Switzerland. [340]

---

[334] Reported in The Guardian, September 3, 2000.

[335] *42 killed by handguns last year*, The Times, January 10, 2001, reporting on statistics supplied by the British Home Office.

[336] *Illegal Firearms in the UK*, Centre for Defense Studies at King's College in London, July 2001.

[337] Ibid.

[338] *Crime and Society in England 1750-1900*, Clive Emsley, 1987, at 36.

[339] *Where Kids and Guns Do Mix*, Stephen P. Halbrook, Wall Street Journal, June 1999.

[340] Ibid.

Fact: "… the scale of gun crime in the capital [London] has forced senior officers to set up a specialist unit to deal with ... shootings."[341]

MYTH: GUN CONTROL IN AUSTRALIA IS CURBING CRIME

Fact: Crime has been rising since enacting a sweeping ban on private gun ownership. In the first two years after Australian gun-owners were forced to surrender 640,381 personal firearms, government statistics showed a dramatic increase in criminal activity.[342] In 2001-2002, homicides were up another 20%.[343]

From the inception of firearm confiscation to March 27, 2000, the numbers are:

- Firearm-related murders were up 19%

- Armed robberies were up 69%

- Home invasions were up 21%

The sad part is that in the 15 years before the national gun confiscation:

- Firearm-related homicides dropped nearly 66%

- Firearm-related deaths fell 50%

Fact: Gun crimes have been rising throughout Australia since guns were banned. In Sydney alone, robbery rates with guns rose 160% in 2001, more in the previous year.[344]

Fact: A ten year Australian study has concluded that firearm confiscation had no effect on crime rates.[345] A separate report also concluded that Australia's 1996 gun control laws "found [no] evidence for an impact of the laws on the pre-existing decline in firearm homicides"[346] and yet another report from Australia for a similar time period indicates the same lack of decline in firearm homicides [347]

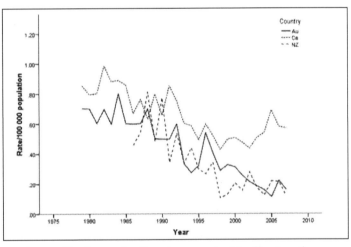

---

[341] Associated News Media, April 30, 2001.

[342] *Crime and Justice - Crimes Recorded by Police*, Australian Bureau of Statistics, 2000.

[343] *Report #46: Homicide in Australia, 2001-2002*, Australian Institute of Criminology, April 2003.

[344] *Costa targets armed robbers*, The Sydney Morning Herald, April 4, 2002.

[345] *Gun Laws and Sudden Death: Did the Australian Firearms Legislation of 1996 Make a Difference?*, Dr. Jeanine Baker and Dr. Samara McPhedran, British Journal of Criminology, November 2006.

[346] *Austrian firearms: data require cautious approach*, S. McPhedran, S. McPhedran, and J. Baker, The British Journal of Psychiatry, 2007, 191:562

Fact: Despite having much stricter gun control than New Zealand (including a near ban on handguns) firearm homicides in both countries track one another over 25 years, indicating that gun control is not a control variable.[348]

MYTH: JAPAN HAS STRICT GUN CONTROL AND A LESS VIOLENT SOCIETY

Fact: In Japan, the total murder rate is almost 1 per 100,000. In the U.S., there are about 3.2 murders per 100,000 people each year by weapons other than firearms.[349] *This means that even if firearms in the U.S. could be eliminated, the U.S. would still have three times the murder rate of the Japanese.*

MYTH: GUN BANS ELSEWHERE WORK

Fact: Though illegal, side-street gun makers thrive in the Philippines, primarily hand crafting exact replicas of submachine guns, which are often the simplest type of gun to manufacture. Estimates are that almost half of all guns in the Philippines are illegal.[350]

Country	Homicides per 100,000 population	
Colombia	62	
Jamaica	32	
Russia	20	
Mexico	13	
Estonia	10	
Latvia	10	
Lithuania	10	
Belarus	9	
Papua New Guinea	8	
Kyrgyzstan	8	

Fact: Chinese police destroyed 113 illegal gun factories and shops in a three-month crackdown in 2006. Police seized 2,445 tons of explosives, 4.81 million detonators and 117,000 guns.[351]

MYTH: THE UNITED STATES HAS THE HIGHEST VIOLENCE RATE BECAUSE OF LAX GUN CONTROL

Fact: The top 10 countries for homicide do not include the U.S.[352]

---

[347] *Australian firearms legislation and unintentional firearm deaths a theoretical explanation for the absence of decline following the 1996 gun laws Public Health*, Samara McPhedran, Jeanine Baker, Public Health, Volume 122, Issue 3

[348] *Firearm Homicide in Australia, Canada, and New Zealand: What Can We Learn From Long- Term International Comparisons?*, Samara McPhedran, Jeanine Baker, and Pooja Singh, Journal of Interpersonal Violence, March 16, 2010

[349] Japan data: *1996 Demographic Yearbook*, United Nations, 1998; US data: FBI Uniform Crime Statistics, 1996.

[350] *Filipino gunsmiths are making a killing*, Taipei Times, May 7, 2005.

[351] China Radio International Online, September 7, 2006.

[352] United Nations Office on Drugs and Crime, Centre for International Crime Prevention, Seventh United Nations Survey of Crime Trends and Operations of Criminal Justice Systems, covering the period 1998 – 2000.

MYTH: THE UNITED STATES IS THE SOURCE OF 90% OF DRUG SYNDICATE GUNS IN MEXICO

Fact: This is an often misquoted data point from the BATFE, who said 90% of the firearms that have been *interdicted in transport* to Mexico or recovered in Mexico came from the United States. Thus the 90% number includes only the firearms American and Mexican police stop in transport.[353]

Fact: The original 90% number was derived from the number of firearms successfully traced, not the total number of firearms criminally used. For 2007-2008, Mexican officials recovered approximately 29,000 firearms from crime scenes and asked for BATFE traces of 11,000. Of those, the BATFE could trace roughly 6,000 of which 5,114 were confirmed to have come from the United States. Thus, 83% of the crime guns recovered in Mexico have not been or cannot be traced to America and the real number is most likely 17%.[354]

Fact: Mexican drug syndicates can buy guns anywhere. For the relatively underpowered civilian rifles coming from the United States, drug runners would pay between 300% and 400% above the market price. Thus they can and are buying guns around the world.[355]

Fact: Mexican drug cartels – with $40 billion in annual revenues – have military armament that includes hand grenades, grenade launchers, armor-piercing munitions, antitank rockets and assault *rifles* smuggled in from Central American countries.[356] These are infantry weapons bought from around the world and not civilian rifles from the United States.

MYTH: MEXICO SEIZES 2,000 GUNS A DAY FROM THE UNITED STATES

Fact: The Mexican attorney general's office reports seizing a total of 29,000 weapons in all of 2007 and 2008, or about 14,500 weapons a year. And that is *all* types of weapons, regardless of country of origin.[357] Had they actually seized approximately 2,000 weapons per day, the total number of seized guns would be closer to 1,460,000.

MYTH: THOUSANDS OF GUNS GO INTO MEXICO FROM THE U.S. EVERY DAY

Fact: In Senate Committee testimony, the BAFTE said the number was likely at worst to be in the "hundreds".[358] As evidenced above, for 2007 and 2008, the average for all firearms seizures was closer to 40 per day (29,000 guns/730 days), and only a fraction of these came from the USA by any means.

---

[353] *Mexico's Massive Illegal weapons coming from China and the U.S.*, American Chronicle, March 14, 2009

[354] *The Myth of 90 Percent*, Fox News, April 2, 2009, BATFE data distilled by William La Jeunesse and Maxim Lott

[355] *Southwest Border Region--Drug Transportation and Homeland Security Issues*, National Drug Intelligence Center, October 2007

[356] *Drug cartels' new weaponry means war*, Los Angeles Times, March 15, 2009

[357] *The Myth of 90 Percent*, William La Jeunesse and Maxim Lott, Fox News, April 2, 2009

[358] Senate Committee Judiciary, William Hoover, Assistant Director, Bureau of Alcohol, Tobacco, & Firearms, March 17, 2009

LICENSING AND REGISTRATION

MYTH: OTHER COUNTRIES REGISTER GUNS TO FIGHT CRIME

Fact: Most of these laws were enacted in the post World War I period to prevent civil uprisings as had occurred in Russia. A report of "Committee on the Control of Firearms," written by British Home Office officials in 1918, was the basis for registration in the U.K., Australia, Canada, and New Zealand.[359]

Fact: Though restrictions were few in the United States and the number of legally held handguns exceeded those on the Canadian side by a factor of ten, rates of homicide were virtually identical.[360]

Fact: Even so, it does not prevent gun crimes. In a one week period, a licensed gun owner killed 12 people in England[361] and a Chinese security guard killed three judges in a court building[362] despite complete licensing and registration.

MYTH: GUN REGISTRATION WORKS

Fact: Not in <u>California</u>. California has had handgun registration since 1909[363] and it has not had any impact on violent crime rate.[364]

Fact: Not in <u>New Zealand</u>. They repealed their gun registration law in the 1980s after police acknowledged its worthlessness.[365]

Fact: Not in <u>Australia</u>. One report states, "It seems just to be an elaborate system of arithmetic with no tangible aim. Probably, and with the best of intentions, it may have been thought, that if it were known what firearms each individual in Victoria owned, some form of control may be exercised, and those who were guilty of criminal misuse could be readily identified. This is a fallacy, and has been proven not to be the case."[366] In addition, cost to Australian taxpayers exceeded $200 million annually.[367]

---

[359] *Response to Philip Alpers' submission to the California State Assembly Select Committee on Gun Violence,* Steven W. Kendrick, January 2000.

[360] American Journal of Epidemiology, Brandon Centrewall, Volume 134, Page 1245-65. Though the rate of homicides as a whole were different, when demographics between the two cities were equalized, the homicide rates matched.

[361] *Gun control and ownership laws in the UK,* BBC, June 3, 2010

[362] *Man shoots dead three judges in China court,* Bangkok Post, June 1, 2010

[363] In conversation between the author of *Gun Facts* and a representative of California Department of Justice.

[364] FBI, Uniform Crime Reports, via the *Data Online* data analysis tool on the website of the Bureau of Justice Statistics.

[365] Background to the Introduction of Firearms User Licensing Instead of Rifle and Shotgun Registration Under the Arms Act 1983, (Wellington, New Zealand: n.p., 1983)

[366] Registration Firearms System, Chief Inspector Newgreen, CRB File 39-1-1385/84

[367] *The Failed Experiment: Gun Control and Public Safety in Canada, Australia, England and Wales,* Gary Mauser, The Fraser Institute, 2003.

Fact: Not in <u>Canada</u>. More than 20,000 Canadian gun-owners have publicly refused to register their firearms. Many others (as many as 300,000[368]) are silently ignoring the law.

- The provincial governments of Alberta, Saskatchewan, and Manitoba have dumped both the administration and the enforcement of all federal gun-control laws right back into Ottawa's lap, throwing the Canadian government into a paper civil war.

- And all at a cost more than 1,646% the original projected cost[369] (the original cost was estimated at 5% of all police expenditures in Canada[370]). "The gun registry as it sits right now is causing law abiding citizens to register their guns but it does nothing to take one illegal gun off the street or to increase any type of penalty for anybody that violates any part of the legislation," according to Al Koenig, President, Calgary Police Association.[371] "We have an ongoing gun crisis, including firearms-related homicides lately in Toronto, and a law registering firearms has neither deterred these crimes nor helped us solve any of them," according to Toronto police Chief Julian Fantino .[372]

- The system is so bad that six Canadian provinces (British Columbia, Manitoba, Saskatchewan, Alberta, Nova Scotia, and Ontario) are refusing to prosecute firearm owners who fail to register.[373]

- A bill to abolish the registry has been tabled (introduced) in the Canadian Parliament, which if passed, would eliminate the registry completely.[374]

- A Saskatchewan MP who endorsed the long gun registry when first proposed has introduced legislation to abolish it stating that, "[the registry] has not saved one life in Canada, and it has been a financial sinkhole … absolutely useless in helping locate the 255,000 people who have been prohibited from owning firearms by the courts."[375]

Fact: Not in <u>Germany</u>. The Federal Republic of Germany began comprehensive gun registration in 1972. The government estimated that between 17,000,000 and 20,000,000 guns were to be registered, but only 3,200,000 surfaced, leaving 80% unaccounted for.[376]

Fact: Not in <u>Boston, Cleveland, or California</u>. These cities and state require registration of "assault weapons." The compliance rate in Boston and Cleveland is about 1%.[377]

---

[368] Standing Committee on Justice and Human Rights, Evidence number 55, June 5, 2003

[369] *Ottawa Under Pressure Over Gun Registry Fiasco*, David Ljunggren, Reuters, December 4, 2002.

[370] *When 'Gun Control' costs lives*, John Lott, Firing Line, September 2001.

[371] Calgary Herald, September 1, 2000.

[372] *Opponents increase pressure to halt Canada's gun control program*, Associated Press, Jan 3, 2002.

[373] *Victoria won't enforce firearms act*, Vancouver Sun, June 06, 2003.

[374] *An Act to amend the Criminal Code and the Firearms Act*, Received first reading June 19, 2006.

[375] *$2 billion worth of police will save more lives than one gun registry*, Garry Breitkreuz, National Post, February 27, 2009.

[376] *Why Gun Registration will Fail*, Ted Drane, Australian Shooters Journal, May 1997.

[377] *The Samurai, the Mountie, and the Cowboy: Should America Adopt the Gun Controls of Other Democracies*, David B. Kopel, 231, n.210 (1992).

Fact: Criminals don't register their guns, nor are they legaly required to do so.[378]

MYTH: GUN REGISTRATION WILL HELP POLICE FIND SUSPECTS

Fact: Registration is required in Hawaii, Chicago and Washington DC. Yet there has not been a single case where registration was instrumental in identifying someone who committed a crime.[379] Criminals very rarely leave their guns at the scene of the crime. Would-be criminals also virtually never get licenses or register their weapons.

MYTH: REGISTRATION DOES NOT LEAD TO CONFISCATION

Fact: It did in Canada. The handgun registration law of 1934 was the source used to identify and confiscate (without compensation) over half of the registered handguns in 2001.[380]

Fact: It did in Germany. The 1928 Law on Firearms and Ammunition (before the Nazis came into power) required all firearms to be registered. When Hitler came into power, the existing lists were used for confiscating weapons.

Fact: It did in Australia. In 1996, the Australian government confiscated over 660,000 previously legal weapons from their citizens.

Fact: It did in California. The 1989 Roberti-Roos Assault Weapons Control Act required registration. Due to shifting definitions of "assault weapons," many legal firearms are now being confiscated by the California government.

Fact: It did in New York City. In 1967, New York City passed an ordinance requiring a citizen to obtain a permit to own a rifle or shotgun, which would then be registered. In 1991, the city passed a ban on the private possession of some semi-automatic rifles and shotguns, and "registered" owners were told that those firearms had to be surrendered, rendered inoperable, or taken out of the city.

Fact: It did in Bermuda, Cuba, Greece, Ireland, Jamaica, and Soviet Georgia as well.

MYTH: LICENSING WILL KEEP BAD PEOPLE FROM OBTAINING OR USING GUNS

Fact: Not in Canada. Canadian homicide rates were virtually unchanged before and after gun registration requirements were implemented (151/100,000 people in 1998 and 149/100,000 in 2002).[381]

Fact: In New York State alone, approximately 100,000 persons are convicted of unlicensed operation of a motor vehicle each year, and this is probably a small proportion of the actual number of people who drive without a valid license.[382] Licensing requirements don't stop ineligible people from driving, and they do not stop ineligible people from acquiring guns.

---

[378] Haynes v. United States

[379] *Gun Licensing Leads to Increased Crime, Lost Lives,* John Lott, L.A. Times, Aug 23, 2000.

[380] *Civil Disobedience In Canada: It Just Happened To Be Guns,* Dr. Paul Gallant, and Dr. Joanne Eisen, Idaho Observer, August 2000,

[381] Statistics Canada, Oct 1, 2003.

[382] Journal of Criminal Law and Criminology, Northwestern University School of Law, 1998.

Fact: As long as the unlicensed purchaser is never caught with the handgun, the unlawful sale will go unnoticed. The risk of detection is negligible. If the unlicensed handgun owner is arrested, he could claim that he did not need a license because he had owned this handgun before licensing went into effect.[383]

Fact: Currently, federal prosecutors do not eagerly accept felon-in-possession cases for prosecution unless the felon is a hardened criminal who represents a threat to the public.[384]

Fact: According to the Supreme Court, criminals do not have to obtain licenses or register their weapons, as that would be an act of self-incrimination.[385]

Fact: Prohibition (which started as a 'moderation' movement) didn't keep people from drinking. Instead it turned millions of otherwise honest and sober citizens into criminals, overnight.

Fact: Most police do not see the benefit. "It is my belief that [licensing and registration] significantly misses the mark because it diverts our attention from what should be our common goal: holding the true criminals accountable for the crimes they commit and getting them off the street."[386]

Fact: In 2005, agencies reported 1,400 arrests of persons denied a firearm or permit; but the U.S. Department of Justice accepted only 135 of those denial cases for prosecution.[387] Given the poor performance of the Federal government in prosecuting felons identified by an instant background check trying to buy firearms, there is little to support firearm licensing as a crime prevention measure.

MYTH: GUNS FROM THE U.S. CREATE CRIME IN OTHER COUNTRIES

Fact: Canada, which shares the longest and most open border with the U.S., doesn't think so, saying that guns from the U.S. are a "small part" of the problem.[388]

---

[383] Ibid.

[384] *Old Chief v. United States: Stipulating Away Prosecutorial Accountability,* Daniel C. Richman, 83 Va. L. Rev. 939, 982-85 (1997).

[385] Haynes vs. U.S. 390 U.S. 85, 1968.

[386] *When 'Gun Control' costs lives,* Bob Brooks, Firing Line, September 2001.

[387] *Background Checks for Firearm Transfers 2005,* U.S. Department of Justice, Office of Justice Programs, November 2006.

[388] Globe and Mail, Paul Culver, August 15, 2005.

MICROSTAMPING

Background: Microstamping is a proposed means for imprinting unique serial numbers onto cartridges fired from a gun. Similar to "ballistic fingerprinting," it allegedly helps police identify what firearm might have been used in a crime. Microstamping uses precision equipment to remove microscopic amounts of metal from the tip of the firing pin

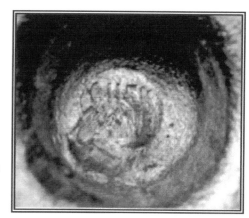

Micro stamped Serial Number

MYTH: INDEPENDENT TESTING BY FORENSIC TECHNOLOGISTS SHOWS THE TECHNOLOGY IS RELIABLE

Fact: Firing pins are readily removable and swappable in most models of handguns, and with inexpensive replacement parts. Criminals who file down serial numbers on the sides of guns won't hesitate to file or exchange firing pins.

Fact: 46% of impressions ranked as "unsatisfactory" (i.e., illegible) after only ten rounds.[389]

Fact: Reloaded ammo (which is extremely common due to the economics of recycling casings and home reloading tools) will make prosecuting cases nearly impossible once the "reloaded ammo" defense is raised (for microstamping that imprints case sides). A *case* may have two or more markings, making the final shooter impossible to identify.

MYTH: FILING THE FIRING PIN WILL MAKE THE GUN INOPERABLE

Fact: Firing pins are designed to be pushed deeply into the primer (igniter) of the round. The depth of the engraving (approximately 0.005 inch)[390] is vastly smaller than the tolerance of the firing pins drive depth.

Fact: In a test, the engravings were removed using a 50-year-old knife sharpening stone in less than a minute. The firearm still operated correctly after the filing.[391]

MYTH: THE COST PER FIREARM WILL BE CHEAP

Fact: The National Shooting Sports Foundation, the representative for firearm manufactures, estimates the cost will be upwards of $150 per firearm, more than tripling the price of self-protection and making it unaffordable for low-income people.[392] The Brady Campaign dispute those with firearm manufacturing experience claiming micro-stamping would cost only 50¢?

---

[389] *NanoTag™ Markings From Another Perspective*, George G. Krivosta, Suffolk County Crime Laboratory, Hauppauge, New York, Winter 2006 edition of the AFTE Journal

[390] Ibid

[391] Ibid

[392] *Etched bullets interest law enforcement*, The Record, September 25, 2006

MYTH: THE NUMBERS WILL LET POLICE FIND THE GUN'S OWNER AND HELP SOLVE CRIMES

Fact: Since many crime guns are stolen property, [393] finding the original owner does not help solve the crime.

---

[393] *Armed and Considered Dangerous*, U.S. Department of Justice, 1986

.50-CALIBER RIFLES

MYTH: .50-CALIBERS ARE THE FAVORITE WEAPON OF TERRORISTS

Fact: Most terrorist attacks are in the form of bombings (90%). Other acts, such as kidnapping (6%), armed attack (2%), arson (1%), firebombing (1%), and other methods (2%), are far less common.[394] Of the "armed attacks," the most common weapons used are fully-automatic AK-47 rifles.

Fact: A single .50 caliber rifle costs upwards of $10,000, yet terrorists can buy the favored AK-47 in Pakistan for less than $200. History shows they opt for the AK-47.

Fact: .50-caliber rifles are heavy (20-35 pounds), expensive (from $3,000 to $10,000 each, with ammunition costing $2-$5 for each round), impossible to conceal (typically four feet long), usually single shot (slow to reload), and impractical for terrorists.

Fact: .50-caliber rifles have only been used in 18 crimes in the history of the United States.[395]

MYTH: AMERICAN GUN MAKERS SOLD .50-CALIBERS TO TERRORISTS

Fact: This "study" by the anti-gun Violence Policy Center was inaccurate. The rifles in question were sold to the United States government. Years later, the U.S. government gave the rifles to Afghan freedom fighters to defeat the former Soviet Union. There is no direct connection between gun makers and terrorists, and none of the rifles have been used in terrorist actions.[396]

MYTH: .50-CALIBER SHOOTERS ARE TERRORISTS IN TRAINING

Fact: The average .50-caliber enthusiast is a successful businessman with an annual income of $50,000 or more – hardly a terrorist profile.[397]

MYTH: THE FOUNDING FATHERS WOULD HAVE HAD NO USE FOR A .50-CALIBER RIFLE

Fact: Common guns of the early American republic were larger than .50-caliber, many measuring up to .812 caliber. The famous Kentucky Rifle (a name eventually given to most rifles made by German immigrants) was usually between .60 to .75-caliber.

---

[394] *Facts and Figures About Terrorism*, Dexter Ingram, Heritage Foundation, September 14, 2001 (some attacks had multiple methods which accounts for a total in excess of 100%).

[395] *Weaponry: .50 Caliber Rifle Crime*, General Accounting Office Report number OSI-99-15R, revised Oct. 21, 2001.

[396] Barret Manufacturing letter on their web site available January 12, 2001. This was confirmed during a visit by the BATF according to Dave Kopel in a National Review article "Guns and (Character) Assassination", December 21, 2001.

[397] John Burtt, Fifty Caliber Shooters Policy Institute, Congressional testimony

---

Myth: .50-calibers are capable of piercing airline fuel tanks from a mile away

Fact: Most expert long distance shooters cannot hit a stationary target under perfect, windless conditions at such distances (one notable exception in Vietnam[398]). Ill-trained terrorists shooting a high-recoil .50-caliber rifle at fast moving targets – a 280 mph airplane – have no chance.

Fact: The only known uses of .50-caliber weapons in downing aircraft have been military aircraft using *fully-automatic machine guns* spraying fire while in combat against other aircraft, and as sniper fire on *stationary aircraft* (i.e., on the ground) on enemy airfields. Not even the military's best sharp shooters are going to ignite a jet's fuel tank when the jet is flying between 200-300 miles per hour.

Myth: .50-caliber bullets can penetrate concrete bunkers

Fact: "It takes 300 rounds to penetrate 2 meters of reinforced concrete at 100 meters."[399] At $5 per round, it would cost a terrorist $1,500 in ammunition to shoot into one bunker.

Myth: .50-caliber bullets can pierce light armor at 4 miles[400]

Fact: "At 35 meters distance [0.5% of the mythical "four mile" distance], a .50-caliber round will go through one inch armor plate."[401] Piercing any armor at four miles is highly improbable.

Fact: "It is exceedingly difficult to hit a target, even a large one … at anything over 1200 to 1500 yards by even highly trained individuals ... The ammo is designed for a machine gun, and is generally only good for 2-3 minute of angle [fraction of a degree] of accuracy. That equates to a 30-45 inch circle at 1500 yards with a perfect rifle, no wind or other conditions and a trained shooter."[402]

Myth: .50-caliber rifles can knock a helicopter from the sky

Fact: The terminal energy of a .50-caliber (6,000 ft-lbs) is not enough to knock a modern military aircraft from the sky unless it hits a critical component like a fuel line. Records exist showing this has been done with common, smaller caliber assault rifles such as AK-47s.

Myth: .50-caliber guns are for snipers

Fact: Americans have been long-distance target shooters since revolutionary times. According to period writings, Americans were shooting small targets at upwards of 150 yards

---

[398] *One Shot, One Kill: American Combat Snipers in World War II, Korea, Vietnam, Beirut*, C. Sasser and C. Roberts, Pocket Books , referring to Marine sniper Carlos Hathcock.

[399] *An Infantryman's Guide to Combat in Built-up Area*, field manual 90-10-1, US Army, May 1993.

[400] Senator Dianne Feinstein, Senate testimony, March 9, 2001.

[401] *An Infantryman's Guide to Combat in Built-up Area*, field manual 90-10-1, US Army, May 1993.

[402] *Ibid.*

using simple Kentucky long rifles and muskets.[403]

Fact: "The use of [.50-caliber] by the IRA in Northern Ireland to shoot both soldiers and police officers at very short range (never more than 275 yards) also gave the weapon a worldwide notoriety when the world's media slapped a 'sniper' label on the terrorists taking the shots. They obviously were not and soon ran scared when professional snipers were deployed to stop them."[404]

---

[403] *Firearms Ownership & Manufacturing in Early America*, Clayton Cramer, unpublished.

[404] *Sniper*, Mark Spicer, Salamander Books, 2001.

ASSORTED MYTHS

MYTH: 30,000 PEOPLE ARE KILLED WITH GUNS EVERY YEAR.

Fact: 54% of these deaths are suicides[405] (80% in Canada[406]). Numerous studies have shown that the presence or absence of a firearm does not change the overall (i.e., gun plus non-gun) suicide rate.

MYTH: THE BRADY CAMPAIGN HAS A GOOD RANKING SYSTEM OF STATE GUN CONTROL LAWS.

Fact: There is zero correlation between the letter grades given by the Brady Campaign and the violent crime or murder rate in those states, making the Brady grade irrelevant (see chart at right).[407]

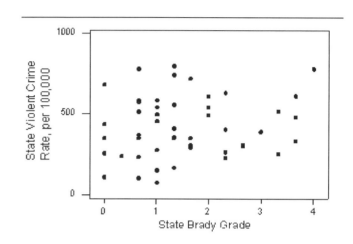

MYTH: 1,000 PEOPLE DIE EACH DAY FROM GUNS

Fact: 25% of this unreliable figure[408] includes "direct war deaths," and another 14% are suicides. The bulk of the rest come from violence-prone and near-lawless localities.

Fact: The source for this raw data admits, "A complete dataset on people killed in conflict—directly or indirectly—does not exist. All published figures are *estimates* based on *incomplete information.*"[409]

Fact: Indeed, the definition of "gun" seems to be very broad: "… revolvers and self-loading pistols, rifles and carbines, assault rifles, sub-machine guns, and light machine guns." Light weapons are "… heavy machine guns, hand-held under-barrel and mounted grenade launchers, portable antitank and anti-aircraft guns, recoilless rifles, portable launchers of anti-tank and antiaircraft missile systems, and mortars of less than 100mm caliber." And they admit to the problem of a broad definition: "The Survey uses the terms 'small arms,' 'firearms,' and 'weapons,' interchangeably. Unless the context dictates otherwise, no distinction is intended between commercial firearms (e.g. hunting rifles), and small arms and light weapons designed for military use (e.g. assault rifles)."[410]

---

[405] National Center for Health Statistics, average rates for years 1981 through 2003.

[406] *Death Involving Firearms*, Kathryn Wilkins, Health Report vol. 16, no 4, Statistics Canada.

[407] *State Got a Poor 'Brady Gun Grade?' Don't Rush to Pack Your Bags*, Denton Bramwell, 2006.

[408] *Bringing the global gun crisis under control*, IANSA, 2006 citing Small Arms Survey.

[409] Small Arms Survey 2005, www.smallarmssurvey.org.

[410] Small Arms Survey 2002, www.smallarmssurvey.org.

Myth: High capacity guns lead to more deadly shootings

Fact: Much of this myth comes from the fact that the general availability of high-capacity handguns briefly preceded the rise in the crack cocaine trade, which brought a new kind of violence in local drugs wars.[411]

Fact: The number of shots fired by criminals has not changed significantly even with the increased capacity of handguns and other firearms. Indeed, the number of shots from revolvers (all within 6-8 round capacity) and semi-automatics were about the same – 2.04 vs. 2.53.[412] In a crime or gun battle, there is seldom time or need to shoot more.

Fact: Fatal criminal shootings declined from 4.3% to 3.3% from 1974 through 1995, when the increase in semi-automatics and large capacity handguns were rising at their fastest rate.[413] Fatal shootings of police officers declined sharply from 1988 through 1993.[414]

Fact: Drug dealers tend to be "more deliberate in their efforts to kill their victims by shooting them multiple times."[415]

Myth: The "powerful gun industry" stops all gun control legislation

Fact: The firearms industry is composed of "small, marginally profitable companies," with combined revenues of $1.5 billion to $2 billion per year, making it politically ineffective.[416]

Fact: Total political contributions from firearm industry members, PACs and employees was under $4.4 million in the 2002 election cycle, which made the industry the 64th ranked contributor. Compare that to $33 million from the American Federation of State, County & Municipal Employees.[417]

Fact: Perhaps the "gun industry" being referenced is the 100+ million adults who peacefully own firearms and do not want their civil rights restricted.

---

[411] *Targeting Guns*, Gary Kleck, 1997.

[412] *Urban firearm deaths: A five-year perspective*, Michael McGonigal, John Cole, William Schwab, Donald Kauder, Michael Rotondo, Peter Angood, Journal of Trauma, 1993.

[413] FBI Uniform Crime Statistics, 1966-1995.

[414] *Firearm injury from crime*, Marianne Zawitz, 1996, Bureau of Justice Statistics.

[415] *Epidemiological changes in gunshot wounds in Washington D.C*, Webster, Champion, Gainer and Sykes, Archives of Surgery, 1992.

[416] New York Times, Mar. 18, 2000.

[417] OpenSecrets.org, May 2003.

MYTH: ACCESS TO GUNS INCREASES THE RISK OF SUICIDE

Fact: The rate of suicide is not affected by the presence of a firearm. This is true in either a time-series analysis (like the chart at right showing the change in handgun supply in the U.S. over time),[418] or through cross-national analysis. For example, Japan has no private handgun ownership (aside from an extremely limited number of licensed Olympic sport shooters), and yet had a suicide rate more than twice that of the United States in 2002.[419]

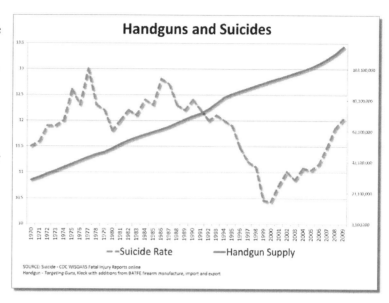

MYTH: INDIVIDUALS WHO COMMIT SUICIDE ARE MORE LIKELY TO HAVE HAD ACCESS TO GUNS[420]

Fact: This is a classic causal effect. If someone decides to commit suicide, and they choose to use a gun, they will first acquire a gun. As noted before, the total rate of suicide does not change when a gun is present because the victim will choose a different method.

MYTH: THE ONLY PURPOSE FOR A GUN IS TO KILL PEOPLE

Fact: Guns are used for self-defense 2,500,000 times a year in the United States.[421]

Fact: Guns are used as a deterrent to crime even when no rounds are fired.[422]

Fact: Guns are used in sports including hunting, target practice, practical pistol, scenario simulation, skeet, etc.

---

[418] FBI Uniform Crime Statistics online, BATFE Firearm Commerce Report for 2002.

[419] FBI Uniform Crime Statistics, World Health Organization Suicide Prevention country reports (online).

[420] *Mental Illness, Previous Suicidality, and Access to Guns in the United States*, Ilgen, Zivin, McCammon, Valenstein, 2008 American Psychiatric Association

[421] *Targeting Guns*, Gary Kleck, Aldine Transaction, 1997

[422] Ibid.

GUN OWNERS AND PUBLIC OPINION

MYTH: GUN OWNERS ARE A TINY MINORITY

Fact: The Federal government estimated that there were over 65 million gun owners in the U.S. and more than 50% were handgun owners.[423] This number is generally considered low due to the reluctance of many to admit to a government agency that they own a gun. Other estimates indicate that between 41% and 49% of U.S. households are gun-owning households.

Fact: 43% of Americans claim that they own a gun.[424]

MYTH: PEOPLE DO NOT BELIEVE THAT THE 2ND AMENDMENT IS AN INDIVIDUAL RIGHT

Fact: A Gallup survey confirms that 73% of Americans believe the 2nd Amendment "guarantees" the right to keep guns, and that a mere 20% believe it exists to enable state militias.[425]

Fact: A Zogby poll[426] concluded that 75% of Americans believe the right to keep and bear arms is an individual right. ABC determined the rate to be 77%.[427]

MYTH: MOST AMERICANS FAVOR GUN CONTROL

Fact: Few "surveys" conducted in this country on the subject of gun control are unbiased. Professional survey designers have criticized both Harris and Gallup gun surveys for their construction – that the surveys have been designed to reach a desired conclusion.[428]

Cause of Gun Violence	%
The way parents raise their children	45%
Popular culture	26%
Availability of guns	21%
Other	6%
No opinion	2%

Fact: 2012 annual Gallup Poll reported that 59% of Americans thought gun laws were properly set and 8% wanted them to be less strict.

Fact: Americans believe that parents and popular culture are more responsible for violence in America than firearms.

---

[423] Bureau of Alcohol, Tobacco and Firearms, 1997.

[424] *Americans by Slight Margin Say Gun in the Home Makes It Safer*, Gallup Poll, October 20, 2006.

[425] *Public Believes Americans Have Right to Own Guns*, Gallup Poll, May 27, 2008.

[426] *SAF survey of 1,015 likely voters*, Zogby, June 2002.

[427] ABC News, May 14, 2002.

[428] Often these surveys use questions like "If it reduced crime, would you favor stronger gun control laws?" These questions are rephrased in headline to read "Americans demand gun control" while ignoring the leading goal of reducing crime. These surveys also fail to ask counter balancing questions to prove/disprove any bias in questions. A counter-balancing question might be: "If it were shown that gun control laws were ineffective in preventing crime, would you favor enacting more gun control laws?"

Fact: 52% of Americans in 2006 do not believe more gun control is needed.[429]

Fact: Only 39% believe stricter gun control is needed, down from 43% in an earlier poll.[430]

Fact: An Associated Press poll in April, 2000 showed 42% thought stricter enforcement was more likely to cut gun violence. Only 33% said enacting tougher gun laws was better.

Fact: A survey in April, 2000 by ABC News/Washington Post asked whether "passing stricter gun control laws" or "stricter enforcement of existing laws" is the best way to curb gun violence. Enforcement was preferred by 53% to 33%.

Fact: 58% percent of Americans believe better enforcement of existing laws "is a better way to reduce handgun violence" than new gun control laws.[431]

Fact: A 1999 survey by CBS (hardly a pro gun organization) found these responses:

- Only 14% of Americans believe that gun control can prevent violence with guns.
- 56% of people said enforcement of existing laws is the better way to reduce violent crime than new gun control laws.
- Only 4% said gun control should be a top issue for the government.

Fact: A recent and well-constructed survey by Time Magazine showed some interesting results. From 33,202 adult Americans surveyed in 1998:

	Yes	No
Should the U.S. have stricter gun control laws?	6.73%	92.25%
Do you believe that allowing people to carry concealed weapons reduce crime?	92.22%	7.76%
Do you believe that U.S. cities should sue gun manufacturers to recoup money spent dealing with gun-related crime?	1.96%	98.01%
How would you rate the effectiveness of the Brady Bill and the "assault weapons" ban in preventing the illegal use and distribution of guns?	0.52%	Very effective
	3.79%	Somewhat effective
	6.19%	Somewhat ineffective
	87.27%	Not at all effective
	2.23%	Don't know

---

[429] *Rasmussen Reports*, February 19, 2006.

[430] *Rasmussen Reports*, October 05, 2009

[431] *Portrait of America Survey*, August 2000.

Fact: According to an AOL.com poll in March 2000:

How can gun violence be effectively prevented?	People	Percent
Stricter gun control laws	10,841	17.8%
Proper enforcement of current gun control laws	13,587	22.4%
Ban on handguns	8,008	13.2%
Stricter punishment for crimes involving guns	21,596	35.6%
Other	5,094	8.4%
Not sure	1,613	2.7%

Fact: A CNN survey in the summer of 1999 asked if gun makers should be held liable for gun violence. Obviously not.

Fact: A 1999 survey by the Associated Press showed:

- A plurality (49%) felt enforcing existing laws was the key to reducing violent crime.
- 52% felt that background checks did not help reduce the number of crimes committed with guns.

Fact: A 2000 Zogby telephone survey of 1,201 adults concluded that, by almost a two-to-one margin, Americans prefer enforcement of existing laws instead of new and tougher gun legislation to fight crime. The same poll found that 68% of the public disagrees with cities suing gun makers for the criminal misuse of guns.

Zogby December 2000 Survey	
Enforce existing laws	52%
Banning handguns	15%
Teach children self-control	15%
Additional congressional legislation	2%
Other	8%
Don't know	2%

Fact: A December 2000 Zogby poll of 1,028 American adults showed that they felt enforcing current laws was the "best way to solve gun violence in America."

Fact: A January 2001 Zogby, "American Values," poll found that 66% of voters felt that the U.S. should spend more money enforcing current laws including mandatory jail time for those who commit a crime with a handgun, while only 26% felt there should be more gun control laws including mandatory gun locks.

MYTH: MORE AND MORE AMERICANS SUPPORT STRICTER GUN CONTROL

Fact: The Gallup Poll has been asking Americans this question since 1990 and in the 16 years thereafter, the number supporting stricter gun control has fallen from 78% to 56%.[432]

Fact: Twice as many Americans currently reject the idea of a handgun ban, though a majority favored such a ban in 1959.[433]

---

[432] *Americans by Slight Margin Say Gun in the Home Makes It Safer*, Gallup Poll, October 20, 2006.

[433] *Ibid.*

MYTH: PEOPLE WANT TO BAN HANDGUNS

Fact: Only 29% of Americans believe handguns should be banned from private ownership and this rate is down from 60% when polling began in the 1950's.[434]

MYTH: PEOPLE OPPOSE CONCEALED CARRY

Fact: Ignoring for a moment that 42 states have enacted "shall issue" concealed carry

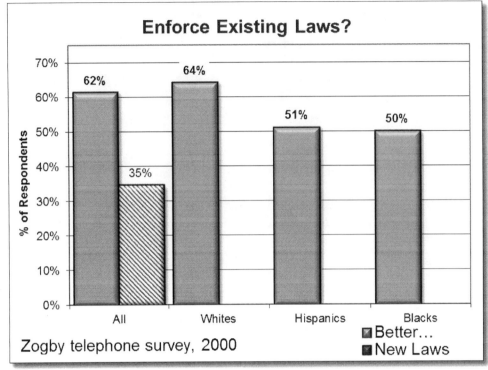

laws (and two more never bothered to outlaw concealed carry), 2009 survey showed 83% support concealed carry laws as they are commonly enacted.[435]

MYTH: MOST PEOPLE THINK GUNS IN THE HOME ARE DANGEROUS

Fact: Gallup poll concludes that a slight majority (47% vs. 43%) believe that having a firearm in the home makes it safer.[436]

MYTH: PEOPLE WANT LOCAL GOVERNMENT TO BAN GUNS

Fact: Only 20% of people believe local gun control is permissible – 69% disagree.[437]

---

[434] *Before Recent Shootings, Gun-Control Support Was Fading*, Gallup Poll, April 8, 2009.

[435] Zogby, August 4, 2009

[436] Ibid.

[437] *Rasmussen Reports*, October 05, 2009

GUN CONTROL PROPONENTS

POLITICIANS

BILL CLINTON, FORMER PRESIDENT OF THE UNITED STATES

"Only the police should have handguns."

"When personal freedom's being abused, you have to move to limit it. That's what we did in the announcement I made last weekend on the public housing projects, about how we're going to have weapon sweeps" [438]

Fact: Wang Jun – son of the late Chinese President Wang Zhen – who is chairman of the China International Trade and Investment Company and President of Polytechnologies Corp., attended a White House coffee with Clinton in February 1996 and was granted a meeting with Commerce Secretary Ronald Brown the next day.

He was also connected to more than $600,000 in illegal campaign contributions to the Democrats, the report said. Polytechnologies is an arms-trading company indicted for trying to smuggle 2,000 Chinese AK-47 assault rifles into the United States and it is the largest of the corporate structures owned by the People's Liberation Army. [439]

V.I. LENIN

"One man with a gun can control 100 without one. ... Make mass searches and hold executions for found arms."

DIANNE FEINSTEIN, U.S. SENATOR FROM CALIFORNIA

"Banning guns addresses a fundamental right of all Americans to feel safe."[440]

"If I could have gotten 51 votes in the Senate of the United States for an outright ban, picking up every one of them; "Mr. and Mrs. America, turn 'em all in," I would have done it."[441]

"The National Guard fulfills the militia mentioned in the Second amendment. Citizens no longer need to protect the states or themselves."

JOSEPH STALIN

"If the opposition disarms, well and good. If it refuses to disarm, we shall disarm it ourselves."

FRANK LAUTENBERG, U.S. SENATOR FROM NEW JERSEY

"We have other legislation that all of you are aware that I have been so active on, with my colleagues here, and that is to shut down the gun shows."[442]

---

[438] *Enough is Enough*, MTV, March 22, 1994

[439] CNN May 24, 1999

[440] Associated Press, November 18, 1993

[441] *60 Minutes*, CBS, February 5, 1995

ADOLF HITLER

"The most foolish mistake we could possibly make would be to allow the subject races to possess arms. History shows that all conquerors who have allowed their subject races to carry arms have prepared their own downfall by so doing."[443]

GISELA KALLENBACH, GERMAN MEMBER OF THE EUROPEAN PARLIAMENT

"We in Europe … do not consider the freedom to buy weapons a human right."[444]

HOWARD METZENBAUM, FORMER U.S. SENATOR

"No, we're not looking at how to control criminals ... we're talking about banning the AK-47 and semi-automatic guns."

CHARLES PASHAYAN, U.S. REPRESENTATIVE FROM CALIFORNIA

"All of this has to be understood as part of a process leading ultimately to a treaty that will give an international body power over our domestic laws."[445]

PETE STARK, U.S. REPRESENTATIVE FROM CALIFORNIA

"If a bill to ban handguns came to the house floor, I would vote for it."[446]

WILLIAM CLAY, U.S. REPRESENTATIVE FROM MISSOURI

" ...we need much stricter gun control, and eventually should bar the ownership of handguns"

JOSEPH BIDEN, U.S. SENATOR FROM DELAWARE

"Banning guns is an idea whose time has come."

JOHN CHAFEE, FORMER U.S. SENATOR FROM RHODE ISLAND

"I shortly will introduce legislation banning the sale, manufacture or possession of handguns (with exceptions for law enforcement and licensed target clubs)... . It is time to act. We cannot go on like this. Ban them!"[447]

JAN SCHAKOWSKY, U.S. REPRESENTATIVE FROM ILLINOIS

"I believe.....this is my final word......I believe that I'm supporting the Constitution of the United States which does not give the right for any individual to own a handgun...."[448]

---

[442] Press conference on March 1, 2000

[443] *Hitler's Secret Conversations*, trans. Norman Cameron and R. H. Stevens, Signet Books, 1961, 403

[444] *EU legislators push together gun controls*, International Herald Tribune, November 29, 2007

[445] United Nations Conference on Small Arms, 2001

[446] Town Hall Meeting, June 1999, Fremont California

[447] *In View of Handguns' Effects, There's Only One Answer: A Ban*, Minneapolis Star Tribune, June 15, 1992, at 13A

[448] Tape recorded on June 25, 2000 by Matt Beauchamp at the Chicago Gay Pride Parade

---

Major Owens, U.S. Representative from New York

"We have to start with a ban on the manufacturing and import of handguns. From there we register the guns which are currently owned, and follow that with additional bans and acquisitions of handguns and rifles with no sporting purpose."

Bobby Rush, U.S. Representative from Illinois

"My staff and I right now are working on a comprehensive gun-control bill. We don't have all the details, but for instance, regulating the sale and purchase of bullets. Ultimately, I would like to see the manufacture and possession of handguns banned except for military and police use. But that's the endgame. And in the meantime, there are some specific things that we can do with legislation." [449]

Ferdinand E. Marcos, Former President/Dictator of the Philippines

President Marcos declared Martial Law by virtue of Proclamation No.1081 on Sept.21, 1972 and on the following day issued General Order No. 6 declaring that no person shall keep, possess or carry any firearms with penalties ranging up to death. The Philippines was under his dictatorship for the next 14 years.

Acts of violence committed by members of gun control organizations

- Barbara Graham, speaker at the "Million Mom March" in 2000, was convicted of shooting and paralyzing for life a man she mistook as one who had killed her son. [450]
- In Fort Collins, a woman who opposes the right of self-defense struck a member of the Tyranny Response Team with a clipboard. [451]
- At a rally in Boulder early in 2000, Robert Howell, vice president of the anti-gun Boulder Bell Campaign, attacked Shariar Ghalam, bloodying his nose. (Ghalam was carrying a concealed handgun but never drew it, not believing his life was in danger.)
- In the summer of 2000, supporters of the anti-gun Million Mom March stole supplies from the Second Amendment Sisters and vandalized SAS property. [452]
- Ari Armstrong, a pro-civil rights activist in Colorado, received threatening telephone calls allegedly from members of S.A.F.E (an anti-gun group) after Ari appeared on television promoting firearm freedoms. [453]

ANTI-FREEDOM POLITICAL ACTIVISTS

The Coalition to Stop Gun Violence

"It is our aim to ban the manufacture and sale of handguns to private individuals." [454]

---

[449] Chicago Tribune, December 5, 1999

[450] *Mother Convicted in Shooting*, Washington Post, February 2, 2001, Page B01 – *Woman Goes on Trial In Ambush Shooting*, January 24, 2001, Page B01

[451] *New gun laws by force*, Boulder Weekly, August 24, 2000

[452] *Million Mom Marchers ransack pro-gun display*, WorldNetDaily, August 1, 2000

[453] Compiled and reported by the Boulder Weekly, August 24, 2000

[454] Recruiting flyer, 1996

"We will never fully solve our nation's horrific problem of gun violence unless we ban the manufacture and sale of handguns and semiautomatic assault weapons."[455]

NELSON T. "PETE" SHIELDS, CHAIRMAN EMERITUS, HANDGUN CONTROL, INC.[456]

" .... the final problem is to make the possession of all handguns and all handgun ammunition except for the military, policemen, licensed security guards, licensed sporting clubs, and licensed gun collectors -- totally illegal."[457]

"Yes, I'm for an outright ban (on handguns)."[458]

"We'll take one step at a time, and the first is necessarily - given the political realities - very modest. We'll have to start working again to strengthen the law, and then again to strengthen the next law and again and again. Our ultimate goal, total control of handguns, is going to take time. The first problem is to slow down production and sales. Next is to get registration. The final problem is to make possession of all handguns and ammunition (with a few exceptions) totally illegal."[459]

SARAH BRADY, CHAIRPERSON FOR HANDGUN CONTROL, INC. (NOW THE BRADY CAMPAIGN)

"...I don't believe gun owners have rights."[460]

"We would like to see, in the future, what we will probably call needs-based licensing of all weapons. ...Where it would make it much more difficult for anybody to be able to purchase handguns...."[461]

"To me, the only reason for guns in civilian hands is for sporting purposes."[462]

JIM BRADY

"[Handguns] For target shooting, that's okay. Get a license and go to the range. For defense of the home, that's why we have police."[463]

ELLIOT CORBETT, SECRETARY, NATIONAL COUNCIL FOR A RESPONSIBLE FIREARMS POLICY

"Handguns should be outlawed."

---

[455] Jeff Muchnick, Legislative Director, USA Today, December 29, 1993

[456] It is interesting to note that HCI was originally named National Council to Ban Handguns.

[457] The New Yorker, July 26, 1976

[458] 60 Minutes interview

[459] New Yorker Magazine, June 26, 1976, pg. 53

[460] *Handguns in America*, Hearst Newspapers Special Report, October 1997

[461] Sarah Brady speech to the Women's National Democratic Club, Sept. 21, 1993

[462] Tampa Tribune, Oct 21, 1993

[463] Parade Magazine, June 26, 1994

BERNARD PARKS, CHIEF OF POLICE, L.A. CALIFORNIA

"We would get rid of assault weapons. There would not be an assault weapon in the United States, whether it's for a show or someone having it in a collection."[464]

JOSH SUGARMANN, EXECUTIVE DIRECTOR OF THE VIOLENCE POLICY CENTER

" ... immediately call on Congress to pass far-reaching industry regulation like the Firearms Safety and Consumer Protection Act ... [which] would give the Treasury Department health and safety authority over the gun industry, and any rational regulator with that authority would ban handguns."[465]

PATRICK V. MURPHY, FORMER NEW YORK CITY POLICE COMMISSIONER

"We are at the point in time and terror where nothing short of a strong uniform policy of domestic disarmament will alleviate the danger which is crystal clear and perilously present. Let us take the guns away from the people."[466]

AMERICAN CIVIL LIBERTIES UNION (ACLU)

"We urge passage of federal legislation ... to prohibit ... the private ownership and possession of handguns."[467]

ROSIE O'DONNELL, TV TALK SHOW HOSTESS

"I think there should be a law -- and I know this is extreme -- that no one can have a gun in the U.S. If you have a gun, you go to jail. Only the police should have guns."[468]

"I don't care if you want to hunt, I don't care if you think it's your right. I say, sorry, you are not allowed to own a gun, and if you do own a gun I think you should go to prison."[469]

VIOLENCE POLICY CENTER

"[gun] Licensing systems are very expensive to administer ... licensing and registration in America would have little effect on the vast majority of gun violence."

"[We are] the largest national gun control advocacy group seeking a ban on handgun production."[470]

ALAN M. DERSHOWITZ, LAWYER AND FRANKFURTER PROFESSOR OF LAW

"The Second Amendment has no place in modern society."[471]

---

[464] Reuters, June 9, 2000

[465] Houston Chronicle, Nov. 5, 1999

[466] Testimony to the National Association of Citizens Crime Commissions

[467] Board of Directors in September 1976 - see national ACLU policy #47

[468] Ottawa Sun, April 29, 1999

[469] The Rosie O'Donnell Show April 19, 1999

[470] *Politics, paranoia fuel war of words over guns*, The Times Union, October 18, 2004

[471] The Crimson Daily, April 9, 2003

BROOKS BROWN, SAFE COLORADO

"It was worth lying to him or deceiving him ..."[472]

THE MEDIA

MICHAEL GARDNER, PRESIDENT OF NBC NEWS

"There is no reason for anyone in this country ... to buy, to own, to have, to use a handgun ...The only way to control handgun use in this country is to prohibit the guns." [473]

"In fact, only police, soldiers -- and, maybe, licensed target ranges -- should have handguns. No one else needs one." [474]

EDITORIAL, LOS ANGELES TIMES

"Why should America adopt a policy of near-zero tolerance for private gun ownership? Because it's the only alternative to the present insanity. Without both strict limits on access to new weapons and aggressive efforts to reduce the supply of existing weapons, no one can be safe."[475]

"...The Times supports a near-total ban on the manufacture and private ownership of handguns and assault weapons, leaving those guns almost exclusively in the hands of law enforcement officials."[476]

JACK E. WHITE, TIME MAGAZINE NATIONAL CORRESPONDENT

"Why not just ban the ownership of handguns when nobody needs one? Why not just ban semi-automatic rifles? Nobody needs one."[477]

GARY WILLS, SYNDICATED COLUMNIST

"Every civilized society must disarm its citizens against each other."[478]

THE MEDIA IN GENERAL

A two-year study by the Media Research Center concluded that television reporters are overwhelmingly opposed to Second Amendment rights. For broadcasts from major networks from July 1, 1995 to June 30, 1997, covering 244 gun policy stories:

- The ratio of anti-gun to pro-gun bias was 16:1.

- Anti-gun spokespeople (Sarah Brady, etc) were given three times the number of sound bites than pro-gun spokespeople (NRA, etc).

---

[472] *SAFE Colorado Says Washington Stunt Was Irresponsible*, The Denver Channel, July 26, 2001, discussing an attempt to influence a congressman on a gun control bill

[473] USA Today, January 16, 1992

[474] The Wall Street Journal, January 10, 1991

[475] *Taming the Monster: Get Rid of the Guns*, Dec. 28, 1993

[476] *Taming the Monster: The Guns Among Us*, Dec. 10, 1993

[477] Washington Times, May 8, 1999

[478] Philadelphia Inquirer, May 17, 1981

THE AMERICAN GOVERNMENT

The following exchange is from the appeal of the case of U.S. vs. Emerson in the Fifth Circuit Court. Meteja was the attorney for the U.S. Government.

Judge Garwood: [to federal lawyer] "You are saying that the Second Amendment is consistent with a position that you can take guns away from the public? You can restrict ownership of rifles, pistols and shotguns from all people? Is that the position of the United States?"

Meteja: [federal lawyer] "Yes"

Garwood: "Is it the position of the United States that persons who are not in the National Guard are afforded no protections under the Second Amendment?"

Meteja: Exactly.

Meteja then said that even membership in the National Guard isn't enough to protect the private ownership of a firearm. It wouldn't protect the guns owned at the home of someone in the National Guard.

Garwood: Membership in the National Guard isn't enough? What else is needed?

Meteja: The weapon in question must be used in the National Guard.

GEORGE NAPPER, ATLANTA PUBLIC-SAFETY COMMISSIONER

"If I had my druthers, the only people who would have guns would be those who enforce the law."[479]

JANET RENO, FORMER U.S. ATTORNEY GENERAL

"The most effective means of fighting crime in the United States is to outlaw the possession of any type of firearm by the civilian populace." [480]

MARION BARRY, FORMER MAYOR, WASHINGTON D.C.

"Our neighbors in Virginia are just as responsible for these killings as the criminals are because they won't pass strong gun [control] legislation."[481] (ed: The claim being that citizens of Virginia were responsible for murders committed in Washington D.C..)

---

[479] U.S. News and World Report

[480] Addressing a 1984 B'nai B'rith gathering in Coral Gables, Florida, per affidavit written by Fred Diamond of Miami.

[481] This Week With David Brinkley, ABC TV, March 19, 1989

GUN CONTROL OPPONENTS

JOHN F. KENNEDY, PRESIDENT OF THE UNITED STATES

"Today, we need a nation of Minutemen, citizens who are not only prepared to take arms, but citizens who regard the preservation of freedom as the basic purpose of their daily life and who are willing to consciously work and sacrifice for that freedom."

"By calling attention to 'a well regulated militia,' the 'security' of the nation, and the right of each citizen 'to keep and bear arms,' our founding fathers recognized the essentially civilian nature of our economy. Although it is extremely unlikely that the fears of governmental tyranny, which gave rise to the Second Amendment, will ever be a major danger to our nation, the Amendment still remains an important declaration of our basic civilian-military relationships, in which every citizen must be ready to participate in the defense of his country. For that reason I believe the Second Amendment will always be important."[482]

MAHATMA GANDHI, PEACEFUL REVOLUTIONARY

"Among the many misdeeds of the British rule in India, history will look upon the Act depriving a whole nation of arms, as the blackest."

ARISTOTLE

"Those who have the command of the arms in a country are masters of the state, and have it in their power to make what revolutions they please. [Thus,] there is no end to observations on the difference between the measures likely to be pursued by a minister backed by a standing army, and those of a court awed by the fear of an armed people."

THE DALAI LAMA

"If someone has a gun and is trying to kill you, it would be reasonable to shoot back with your own gun."[483]

GEORGE ORWELL

"The totalitarian states can do great things, but there is one thing they cannot do: they cannot give the factory-worker a rifle and tell him to take it home and keep it in his bedroom. That rifle, hanging on the wall of the working-class flat or laborer's cottage, is the symbol of democracy. It is our job to see that it stays there."[484]

HUBERT HUMPHREY, FORMER U.S. SENATOR AND VICE PRESIDENT OF THE UNITED STATES

"Certainly one of the chief guarantees of freedom under any government, no matter how popular and respected, is the right of citizens to keep and bear arms.... The right of

---

[482] *Know Your Lawmakers*, Guns Magazine, April 1960, Page 4

[483] *Dalai Lama urges students to shape world*, Seattle Times, May 15, 2001

[484] *Don't Let Colonel Blimp Ruin the Home Guard*, Evening Standard, , Jan 8, 1941

citizens to bear arms is just one guarantee against arbitrary government, one more safeguard against tyranny... "[485]

JOHN ADAMS, PRESIDENT OF THE UNITED STATES

"Resistance to sudden violence, for the preservation not only of my person, my limbs, and life, but of my property, is an indisputable right of nature which I have never surrendered to the public by the compact of society, and which perhaps, I could not surrender if I would."[486]

"Here, every private person is authorized to arm himself, and on the strength of this authority, I do not deny the inhabitants had a right to arm themselves at that time, for their defense, not for offense..."[487]

ST. GEORGE TUCKER, AMERICAN REVOLUTION MAJOR AND POST REVOLUTION JUDGE

"In America we may reasonably hope that the people will never cease to regard the right of keeping and bearing arms as the surest pledge of their liberty."[488]

WALTER MONDALE, FORMER VICE PRESIDENT AND U.S. AMBASSADOR TO JAPAN

"Gun bans don't disarm criminals, gun bans attract them."[489]

THOMAS JEFFERSON, AUTHOR OF THE AMERICAN DECLARATION OF INDEPENDENCE

"No freeman shall be debarred the use of arms (within his own lands or tenements)."[490]

"What country can preserve its liberties if their rulers are not warned from time to time that their people preserve the spirit of resistance. Let them take arms."[491]

"The constitutions of most of our States assert that all power is inherent in the people; that... it is their right and duty to be at all times armed."[492]

"One loves to possess arms, though they hope never to have occasion for them."[493]

"I learn with great concern that [one] portion of our frontier so interesting, so important, and so exposed, should be so entirely unprovided with common fire-arms. I did not suppose any part of the United States so destitute of what is considered as among the first necessaries of a farm-house."[494]

---

[485] *Know Your Lawmakers*, Guns Magazine, Feb 1960, Page 6

[486] Boston Gazette, Sept. 5, 1763

[487] *Legal Papers of John Adams*, Butterfield and Zobel; 1965, opening statement as defense counsel for British soldiers on trial for the Boston Massacre in 1770

[488] American Blackstone, 1803

[489] April 20, 1994

[490] Draft Virginia Constitution (with his note added), Thomas Jefferson, 1776. Papers 1:353

[491] Letter to James Madison, Dec. 20, 1787, in Papers of Jefferson, ed. Boyd et al.

[492] Thomas Jefferson to John Cartwright, 1824. Millennium Edition of The Writings of Thomas Jefferson 16:45

[493] Thomas Jefferson to George Washington, 1796. Millennium Edition of The Writings of Thomas Jefferson 9:341

[494] Thomas Jefferson to Jacob J. Brown, 1808. Millennium Edition of The Writings of Thomas Jefferson 11:432

"None but an armed nation can dispense with a standing army. To keep ours armed and disciplined is therefore at all times important."

JAMES MADISON, AMERICAN FOUNDING FATHER

"[The Constitution preserves] the advantage of being armed which Americans possess over the people of almost every other nation...[where] the governments are afraid to trust the people with arms."

OLIVER STONE, MOVIE DIRECTOR

"I like automatic weapons. I fought for my right to use them in Vietnam."

PATRICK HENRY, AMERICAN FOUNDING FATHER AND CATALYST FOR THE BILL OF RIGHTS

"The great objective is that every man be armed ... . Everyone who is able may have a gun."

MACHIAVELLI

"The Swiss are well armed and enjoy great freedom"[495]

"From this we plainly see the folly and imprudence of demanding a thing, and saying beforehand that it is intended to be used for evil; … For it is enough to ask a man to give up his arms, without telling him that you intend killing him with them; after you have the arms in hand, then you can do your will with them."[496]

TENCHE COXE, REVOLUTIONARY ERA WRITER

"As civil rulers, not having their duty to the people before them, may attempt to tyrannize, and as the military forces which must be occasionally raised to defend our country, might pervert their power to the injury of their fellow citizens, the people are confirmed by the article in their right to keep and bear their private arms."[497]

"Congress have no power to disarm the militia. Their swords, and every other terrible implement of the soldier, are the birthright of an American...   The unlimited power of the sword is not in the hands of either the federal or state government, but, where I trust in God it will ever remain, in the hands of the people"[498]

MALCOLM X, AMERICAN BLACK CIVIL RIGHTS ACTIVIST

"It is criminal to teach a man not to defend himself when he is the constant victim of brutal attacks. It is legal and lawful to own a shotgun or a rifle. We believe in obeying the law." [499]

"... I must say this concerning the great controversy over rifles and shotguns. The only thing I've ever said is that in areas where the government has proven itself either

---

[495] In Switzerland, males age 20 to 42 serving in the army are required to keep rifles or pistols at home

[496] *Discourses on the First Ten Books of Titus Livius*, Niccolò Machiavelli

[497] Remarks on the First Part of the Amendments to the Federal Constitution under the pseudonym 'A Pennsylvanian' in the Philadelphia Federal Gazette, June 18, 1789 at 2 col. 1

[498] Pennsylvania Gazette, Feb. 20, 1788

[499] Statement to the press, March 12, 1964

---

unwilling or unable to defend the lives and the property of Negroes, it's time for Negroes to defend themselves. Article number two of the constitutional amendments provides you and me the right to own a rifle or a shotgun. It is constitutionally legal to own a shotgun or a rifle."[500]

SAMUEL ADAMS, MEMBER OF THE CONTINENTAL CONGRESS

"That the said Constitution shall never be construed to authorize Congress to infringe the just liberty of the press or the rights of conscience; or to prevent the people of The United States who are peaceable citizens from keeping their own arms..."[501]

WILLIAM RAWLE, POST-REVOLUTION U.S. ATTORNEY

"The prohibition is general. No clause in the Constitution could by any rule of construction be conceived to give to Congress a power to disarm the people. Such a flagitious attempt could only be made under some general pretense by a state legislature. But if in any blind pursuit of inordinate power, either should attempt it, this amendment may be appealed to as a restraint on both."[502]

THOMAS PAINE, AMERICAN REVOLUTION POLITICAL PHILOSOPHER

"Arms, like laws, discourage and keep the invader and plunderer in awe and preserve order..."

MAFIA INFORMANT SAMMY "THE BULL" GRAVANO

"Gun control? It's the best thing you can do for crooks and gangsters. I want you to have nothing. If I'm a bad guy, I'm always gonna have a gun. Safety locks? You will pull the trigger with a lock on, and I'll pull the trigger. We'll see who wins."

RICHARD HENRY LEE, MEMBER OF THE CONTINENTAL CONGRESS

"[W]hereas, to preserve liberty, it is essential that the whole body of the people always possess arms, and be taught alike, especially when young, how to use them;"[503]

ALEXANDER HAMILTON, AUTHOR OF THE FEDERALIST PAPERS

"The best we can hope for concerning the people at large is that they be properly armed."[504]

ZACHARIAH JOHNSON

"The people are not to be disarmed of their weapons. They are left in full possession of them."[505]

---

[500] *Malcolm X Speaks*, Merit Publishers, 1965

[501] Debates and Proceedings in the Convention of the Commonwealth of Massachusetts, at 86-87

[502] A View of the Constitution 125-6 (2nd ed. 1829)

[503] Letters from the Federal Farmer to the Republican, at 21,22,124

[504] The Federalist Papers at 184-8

[505] *Debates in the Several State Conventions*, Jonathan Elliot, 646

TIMOTHY DWIGHT, ARMY CHAPLAIN DURING THE AMERICAN REVOLUTION

"To trust arms in the hands of the people at large has, in Europe, been believed...to be an experiment fraught only with danger. Here by a long trial it has been proved to be perfectly harmless...If the government be equitable; if it be reasonable in its exactions; if proper attention be paid to the education of children in knowledge and religion, few men will be disposed to use arms, unless for their amusement, and for the defense of themselves and their country."[506]

CHARLES KRAUTHAMMER, SYNDICATED COLUMNIST

"The Brady Bill's only effect will be to desensitize the public to regulation of weapons in preparation for their ultimate confiscation." [507]

"Passing a law like the assault weapons ban is a symbolic, purely symbolic move. ... Its only real justification is not to reduce crime but to desensitize the public to the regulation of weapons in preparation for their ultimate confiscation."[508]

---

[506] Travels in New England and New York, 1823

[507] The Washington Post, April 5, 1996

[508] Ibid

THE SECOND AMENDMENT

Justification clause: "A well regulated Militia being necessary to the security of a free State,"

Rights clause: "the right of the people to keep and bear Arms shall not be infringed."

The justification clause does not modify, restrict, or deny the rights clause.[509]

For a full discussion of how the 2nd Amendment was created and revised, see "Origin of the 2nd Amendment" in the "Miscellaneous information" section of this book.

MYTH: THE SUPREME COURT RULED THE SECOND AMENDMENT IS NOT AN INDIVIDUAL RIGHT

Fact: In D.C. v Heller the Supreme Court (2008) firmly established the 2nd Amendment is an individual right, as they had in Cruikshank and Dred Scott.

Fact: In McDonald v Chicago (2010) the Supreme Court concluded the right is incorporated against the states via the 14th Amendment.

Fact: Of 300 decisions of the federal and state courts that have taken a position on the meaning of the Second Amendment or the state analogs to it, only 10 have claimed that the right to keep and bear arms is not an individual right. Many of the other decisions struck down gun control laws because they conflicted with the Second Amendment, such as State v. Nunn (Ga. 1846).[510]

Fact: In the Dred Scott case of 1856, the Supreme Court listed the protected rights of citizens and explicitly listed the right to keep and bear arms, and gave this right equal weight to the other freedoms enumerated in the constitution.

MYTH: THE SECOND AMENDMENT IS A COLLECTIVE RIGHT, NOT AN INDIVIDUAL RIGHT

Fact: St. George Tucker, any early legal commentator and authority of the original meaning of the constitution wrote in Blackstone's Commentaries "… nor will the constitution permit any prohibition of arms to the people" [511]

Fact: The Second Amendment was listed in a Supreme Court ruling as an individual right.[512]

Fact: The Supreme Court specifically reaffirmed that the right to keep and bear arms did not belong to the government.[513]

---

[509] Eugene Volokh, Prof. Law, UCLA

[510] *For the Defense of Themselves and the State: The Original Intent and Judicial Interpretation of the Right to Keep and Bear Arms*, Clayton Cramer, Praeger Press, 1994

[511] *Blackstone's Commentaries,* St. GeorgeTucker, Vol 1. Note D. Part 6. Restraints on Powers of Congress (1803).

[512] *Dred Scott, Casey v. Planned Parenthood, U.S. v. Cruikshank* and others

[513] *United States v. Miller*

Fact: In 22 of the 27 instances where the Supreme Court mentions the Second Amendment, they quote the rights clause and not the justification clause.

Fact: Courts disagree. "We find that the history of the Second Amendment reinforces the plain meaning of its text, namely that it protects individual Americans in their right to keep and bear arms whether or not they are a member of a select militia or performing active military service or training" and "We reject the collective rights and sophisticated collective rights models for interpreting the Second Amendment" [514]

Fact: Citizens disagree. 62% believe the 2nd Amendment guarantees an individual right, while a mere 28% believe it protects the power of the states to form militias.[515]

Fact: There are 23 state constitutions with RKBA clauses adopted between the Revolution and 1845, and 20 of them are explicitly individual in nature, only three have "for the common defense...." or other "collective rights" clauses.[516]

Fact: James Madison, considered to be the author of the Bill of Rights, wrote that the Bill of Rights was "calculated to secure the personal rights of the people". He never excluded the Second Amendment from this statement.

Fact: Patrick Henry commented on the Swiss militia model (still in use today) noting that they maintain their independence without "a mighty and splendid President" or a standing army.[517]

Fact: "The congress of the United States possesses no power to regulate, or interfere with the domestic concerns, or police of any state: it belongs not to them to establish any rules respecting the rights of property; nor will the constitution permit any prohibition of arms to the people; or of peaceable assemblies by them, for any purposes whatsoever, and in any number, whenever they may see occasion."[518]

Fact: Tench Coxe, in Remarks on the First Part of the Amendments to the Federal Constitution said: "As civil rulers, not having their duty to the people duly before them, may attempt to tyrannize, and as the military forces which must be occasionally raised to defend our country, might pervert their power to the injury of their fellow-citizens, <u>the people</u> are confirmed by the next article in their right to keep and bear their <u>private arms</u>."

MYTH: THE "MILITIA" CLAUSE IS TO ARM THE NATIONAL GUARD

Fact: "Militia" is a Latin abstract noun, meaning "military service", not an "armed group", and that is the way the Latin-literate Founders used it. To the Romans, "military service" included law enforcement and disaster response. Today "militia" might be more

---

[514] *U.S. v. Emerson*, 5th court of Appeals decision, November 2, 2001, No. 99-10331

[515] Associated Television News Survey, August 1999, 1,007 likely voters

[516] *For the Defense of Themselves and the State: The Original Intent and Judicial Interpretation of the Right to Keep and Bear Arms,* Clayton Cramer, , Praeger Press, 1994, cited as an authority in USA v. Emerson (N.D. Texas 1999)

[517] *Where Kids and Guns Do Mix*, Stephen P. Halbrook, Wall Street Journal, June 2000

[518] *Blackstone's Commentaries,* St. George Tucker, Volume 1   Appendix Note D., 1803 – Tucker's comments provide a number of insights into the consensus for interpretation of the Constitution that prevailed shortly after its ratification, after the debates had settled down and the Constitution was put into practice.

---

meaningfully translated as "defense service", associated with a "defense duty", which attaches to individuals as much as to groups of them, organized or otherwise. When we are alone, we are all militias of one. In the broadest sense, militia is the exercise of civic virtue. [519]

Fact: The Dick Act of 1903 designated the National Guard as the "organized militia" and that all other citizens were the "unorganized militia" – thus the National Guard is only <u>part</u> of the militia, and the whole militia is composed of the population at large. Before 1903, the National Guard had no federal definition as part of the militia at all.

Fact: The first half of the Second Amendment is called the "justification clause". Justification clauses appear in many state constitutions, and cover liberties including right to trial, freedom of the press, free speech, and more. ***Denying gun rights based on the justification clause means we would have to deny free speech rights on the same basis.*** [520] See http://www.law.ucla.edu/faculty/volokh/beararms/testimon.htm

Fact: The origin of the phrase "a well regulated militia" comes from a 1698 treatise "A Discourse of Government with Relation to Militias" by Andrew Fletcher, in which the term "well regulated" was equated with "well-behaved" or "disciplined". [521]

Fact: "We have found no historical evidence that the Second Amendment was intended to convey militia power to the states, limit the federal government's power to maintain a standing army, or applies only to members of a select militia while on active duty. All of the evidence indicates that the Second Amendment, like other parts of the Bill of Rights, applies to and protects individual Americans." [522]

Fact: "The plain meaning of the right of the people to keep arms is that it is an individual, rather than a collective, right and is not limited to keeping arms while engaged in active military service or as a member of a select militia such as the National Guard ..." [523]

Fact: Most of the 13 original states (and many colonies/territories that became states after ratification of the Constitution and before or shortly after ratification of the Bill of Rights) had their own constitutions, and it is from these that the original Bill of Rights was distilled. The state constitutions of that time had many "right to keep and bear arms" clauses that clearly guaranteed an individual right. Some examples include:

> **Connecticut:** Every citizen has a right to bear arms in defense of <u>himself</u> and the state.

> **Kentucky:** … the right of the citizens to bear arms in defense of <u>themselves</u> and the State shall not be questioned.

---

[519] *Militia*, The Constitution Society, www.constiution.org

[520] Eugene Volokh, Prof. Law, UCLA

[521] This document was widely published during the colonial and revolutionary periods, and was the basis for state and federal 'bills of rights'.

[522] *U.S. v. Emerson*, 5th court of Appeals decision, November 2, 2001, No. 99-10331

[523] Ibid

Pennsylvania: That the people have a right to bear arms for the defense of <u>themselves</u> and the state; ... The right of the citizens to bear arms in defense of <u>themselves</u> and the State shall not be questioned.

Rhode Island: The right of the people to keep and bear arms shall not be infringed.

Vermont: … the people have a right to bear arms for the defense of <u>themselves</u> and the State.

MYTH: U.S. V. CRUIKSHANK DENIED AN INDIVIDUAL RIGHT TO BEAR ARMS

Fact: The court ruled that both the 2nd Amendment right to bear arms and the 1st Amendment right to assembly were "pre-existing rights", and that it was incumbent upon the states to enforce that right. Specifically the court ruled:

> *The right was not created by the amendment; neither was its continuance guaranteed, except as against congressional interference. For their protection in its enjoyment, therefore, the people must look to the States. ...*

MYTH: U.S. V. MILLER SAID THAT THE SECOND AMENDMENT IS NOT AN INDIVIDUAL RIGHT

Fact: The Miller case specifically held that specific types of guns might be protected by the Second Amendment. It depended on whether a gun had militia use, and the court wanted evidence presented confirming that <u>citizens have a right to military style weapons</u>. Since no evidence was taken at the trial level in lower courts, they remanded the case for a new trial. Specifically the court said:

> "The signification attributed to the term Militia appears from the debates in the Convention, the history and legislation of Colonies and States, and the writings of approved commentators. *These show plainly enough that the Militia comprised all males physically capable of acting in concert for the common defense.* "A body of citizens enrolled for military discipline." And further, that ordinarily when called for service *these men were expected to appear bearing arms supplied by themselves and of the kind in common use at the time.*"

> "In the absence of any evidence tending to show that possession or use of a 'shotgun having a barrel of less than 18 inches in length' at this time has some reasonable relationship to the preservation or efficiency of a well-regulated militia, we cannot say that the Second Amendment guarantees the right to keep and bear such an instrument. Certainly it is not within judicial notice that this weapon is any part of the ordinary military equipment or that its use could contribute to the common defense."

Fact: Even the US government agreed. Here are some sentences from the brief filed by the government in the appeal to the Supreme Court:

> "The Second Amendment does not grant to the people the right to keep and bear arms, but merely recognizes the prior existence of that right and prohibits its infringement by Congress."

> "The 'arms' referred to in the Second Amendment are, moreover, those which ordinarily are used for military or public defense purposes ..."

"The Second Amendment does not confer upon the people the right to keep and bear arms; it is one of the provisions of the Constitution which, recognizing the prior existence of a certain right, declares that it shall not be infringed by Congress. Thus the right to keep and bear arms is not a right granted by the Constitution and therefore is not dependant upon that instrument for its source."

Fact: The Federal 8th Court of Appeals holds that the Miller case protects an individual right to keep and bear arms. "Although an individual's right to bear arms is constitutionally protected, see United States v. Miller ..."[524]

Fact: Federal courts reject the myth. "We conclude that Miller does not support the [government's] collective rights or sophisticated collective rights approach to the Second Amendment." [525] They continue, "There is no evidence in the text of the Second Amendment, or any other part of the Constitution, that the words 'we the people' have a different connotation within the Second Amendment than when employed elsewhere ...".

SUMMARY OF VARIOUS COURT DECISIONS CONCERNING GUN RIGHTS

DECISIONS THAT EXPLICITLY RECOGNIZED THAT THE SECOND AMENDMENT GUARANTEES AN INDIVIDUAL RIGHT TO PURCHASE, POSSESS OR CARRY FIREARMS, AND IT LIMITS THE AUTHORITY OF BOTH FEDERAL AND STATE GOVERNMENTS:

- Parker vs. D.C., Fed (2007), confirmed an individual right to keep arms and overturning a handgun ban.
- U.S. vs. Emerson, 5 Fed (1999), confirmed an individual right requiring compelling government interest for regulation.
- Nunn v. State, 1 Ga. 243, 250, 251 (1846) (struck down a ban on sale of small, easily concealed handguns as violating Second Amendment).
- State v. Chandler, 5 La.An. 489, 490, 491 (1850) (upheld a ban on concealed carry, but acknowledged that open carry was protected by Second Amendment).
- Smith v. State, 11 La.An. 633, 634 (1856) (upheld a ban on concealed carry, but recognized as protected by Second Amendment "arms there

Court Rulings on the 2nd Amendment

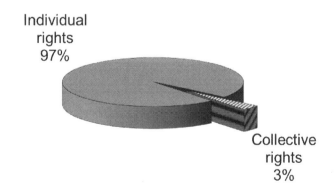

Individual rights 97%

Collective rights 3%

---

[524] *U.S. v. Hutzel*, 8 Iowa, No. 99-3719

[525] *U.S. v. Emerson*, 5th court of Appeals decision, November 2, 2001, No. 99-10331

---

spoken of are such as are borne by a people in war, or at least carried openly").

- State v. Jumel, 13 La.An. 399, 400 (1858) (upheld a ban on concealed carry, but acknowledged a Second Amendment right to carry openly).

- Cockrum v. State, 24 Tex. 394, 401, 402 (1859) (upheld an enhanced penalty for manslaughter with a Bowie knife, but acknowledged that the Second Amendment guaranteed an individual right to possess arms for collective overthrow of the government).

- In Re Brickey, 8 Ida. 597, 70 Pac. 609, 101 Am.St.Rep. 215, 216 (1902) (struck down a ban on open carry of a revolver in Lewiston, Idaho as violating both Second Amendment and Idaho Const. guarantee).

- State v. Hart, 66 Ida. 217, 157 P.2d 72 (1945) (upheld a ban on concealed carry as long as open carry was allowed based on both Second Amendment and Idaho Const. guarantee).

- State v. Nickerson, 126 Mont. 157, 166 (1952) (striking down a conviction for assault with a deadly weapon, acknowledging a right to carry based on Second Amendment and Montana Const. guarantee).

- U.S. v. Hutzell, 8 Iowa, 99-3719, (2000) (cite in dictum that "an individual's right to keep and bear arms is constitutionally protected, see United States v. Miller, 307 U.S. 174, 178-79 (1939).

DECISIONS THAT RECOGNIZED THE SECOND AMENDMENT GUARANTEES AN INDIVIDUAL RIGHT TO POSSESS OR CARRY FIREARMS, BUT ONLY LIMITING THE FEDERAL GOVERNMENT'S AUTHORITY:

- U.S. v. Cruikshank, 92 U.S. 542, 552 (1876) (limiting use of the Enforcement Act of 1870 so that Klansmen could not be punished for mass murder and disarming of freedmen).

- State v. Workman, 35 W.Va. 367, 373 (1891) (upholding a ban on carry of various concealable arms).

- State v. Kerner, 181 N.C. 574, 107 S.E. 222 (1921) (overturning a ban on open carry of pistols based on North Carolina Const., but acknowledging Second Amendment protected individual right from federal laws).

DECISIONS IN WHICH THE SECOND AMENDMENT WAS ARGUED OR RAISED AS A LIMITATION ON STATE LAWS, AND IN WHICH THE COURT RULED THAT IT ONLY LIMITED THE FEDERAL GOVERNMENT, TACITLY ACKNOWLEDGING THAT THE RIGHT WAS INDIVIDUAL IN NATURE:

- Andrews v. State, 3 Heisk. (50 Tenn.) 165, 172, 173 (1871).

- Fife v. State, 31 Ark. 455, 25 Am.Rep. 556, 557, 558 (1876); State v. Hill, 53 Ga. 472, 473, 474 (1874).

- Dunne v. People, 94 Ill. 120, 140, 141 (1879); Presser v. Illinois, 116 U.S. 252, 265, 266 (1886) (upholding a ban on armed bodies marching through the streets).

- People v. Persce, 204 N.Y. 397, 403 (1912); In re Rameriz, 193 Cal. 633, 636, 226 P. 914 (1924) (upholding a ban on resident aliens possessing handguns).

DECISIONS IN WHICH THE SECOND AMENDMENT WAS IMPLIED TO GUARANTEE AN INDIVIDUAL RIGHT, THOUGH UNCLEAR AS TO WHETHER IT LIMITED ONLY THE FEDERAL

GOVERNMENT OR STATES AS WELL, BECAUSE THE TYPE OF ARM IN QUESTION WASN'T PROTECTED:

- English v. State, 35 Tex. 473, 476, 477 (1872).
- State v. Duke, 42 Tex. 455, 458, 459 (1875) (upholding a ban on carrying of handguns, Bowie knives, sword-canes, spears, and brass knuckles).
- People v. Liss, 406 Ill. 419, 94 N.E.2d 320, 322, 323 (1950) (overturning a conviction for carrying a concealed handgun and acknowledging that the right in the Second Amendment was individual).
- Guida v. Dier, 84 Misc.2d 110, 375 N.Y.S.2d 827, 828 (1975) (denying that "concealable hand weapons" were protected by the Second Amendment, but acknowledging that an individual right protects other firearms).

DECISIONS IN WHICH THE SECOND AMENDMENT HAS BEEN CLASSED WITH OTHER INDIVIDUAL RIGHTS, WITH NO INDICATION THAT IT WAS NOT AN INDIVIDUAL RIGHT:

- Robertson v. Baldwin, 165 U.S. 275, 281, 282, 17 S.Ct. 826, 829 (1897); U.S. v. Verdugo-Urquidez, 110 S.Ct. 1056, 1060, 1061 (1990).

DECISIONS THAT COULD HAVE BEEN VERY MUCH SHORTER IF THE COURT HAD SIMPLY DENIED THAT THE SECOND AMENDMENT PROTECTED AN INDIVIDUAL RIGHT:

- U.S. v. Miller, 307 U.S. 174 (1939) (the Supreme Court upholding the National Firearms Act of 1934, after district judge released defendants on the grounds that it violated Second Amendment).

THOUGHTS ON GUN CONFISCATION

In 1911, <u>Turkey</u> established gun control. Subsequently, from 1915 to 1917, 1.5-million Armenians, deprived of the means to defend themselves, were rounded up and killed.

In 1929, the <u>Soviet Union</u> established gun control. Then, from 1929 to 1953, approximately 20-millon dissidents were rounded up and killed.

In 1938 <u>Germany</u> established gun control. From 1939 to 1945 over 13-million Jews, gypsies, homosexuals, mentally ill, union leaders, Catholics and others, unable to fire a shot in protest, were rounded up and killed.

In 1935, <u>China</u> established gun control. Subsequently, between 1948 and 1952, over 20-million dissidents were rounded up and killed.

In 1956, <u>Cambodia</u> enshrined gun control. In just two years (1975-1977) over one million "educated" people were rounded up and killed.

In 1964, <u>Guatemala</u> locked in gun control. From 1964 to 1981, over 100,000 Mayan Indians were rounded up and killed as a result of their inability to defend themselves.

In 1970, <u>Uganda</u> embraced gun control. Over the next nine years over 300,000 Christians were rounded up and killed.

Over 56-million people have died because of gun control in the last century...[526]

Senator Dianne Feinstein, speaking on "60-Minutes" said "if I thought I could get the votes, I'd have taken them all."

SERIOUS QUESTIONS TO ASK YOURSELF

- If guns are effective enough to be a criminal's preferred tool, why are they not good enough to use for protection?

- Why do politicians insist their bodyguards be armed, but not you and me?

- If you and your children were face-to-face with a male attacker twice your size, what *would* you do; If you weren't armed? If you were armed?

- If guns are "too dangerous" to be in our society, then why do our leaders want to be the only ones who have them? Do you trust our leaders implicitly to protect you *at all times*?

- Which is better – more gun control and the eventual banning of all guns in our society, or not sitting by helplessly watching as an intruder repeatedly rapes your 13-year-old daughter?

- If we ever completely ban guns, do you think there would be no more armed criminals in America?

- With so many gun laws already on the books, why do "gun crimes" still exist?

---

[526] (Most of the genocide statistics were reported in:) *Death by 'Gun Control': The Human Cost of Victim Disarmament,"* Aaron Zelman & Richard W. Stevens, 2001.

MISCELLANEOUS STATISTICS

Number of firearms in America: Between 223,000,000[527] and 290,000,000[528]

Number of firearm owning households: At least 50,600,000[529]

Projected firearm owning households in America: 60-85 million

Number of guns used in crimes: 450,000[530]

Percentage of guns used in crimes: 0.09%

MISCELLANEOUS INFORMATION

BRITISH CRIME STATISTICS

The U.K. measures crime using two different processes:

> **British Crime Survey (BCS):** The Home Office conducts surveys of the population to determine how often subjects have been affected by criminal activity. Data is projected to reflect the entire population.

> **Police reporting:** Crimes are reported to the police and nationwide, census-level statistics are summarized.

The BCS has been reporting a declining crime rate in the UK while police reporting has shown an increase. The BCS has routinely been criticized because it <u>under reports</u> crime due to the following factors:

- Murdered and imprisoned people do not answer surveys

- Some crimes are not surveyed when victims are below age 16[531]

- Crime against institutions (bank robbery, etc.) are not included

- Crimes are recorded at final disposition (conviction/acquittal), leaving many crimes completely unreported[532]

These deficiencies are so significant that even the British government does not believe the accuracy of the BCS.

> [T]he BCS did not record 'various categories of violent crime', including murder and rape, retail crime, drug-taking, or offences in which the victims

---

[527] *Guns Used in* Crime, Bureau of Justice Statistics, Marianne W. Zawitz, 1995.

[528] *Small Arms Survey*, Graduate Institute of International Studies, 2008

[529] Surveys show a "reported" ownership rate of 46%, but it is universally believed that these surveys under-reported (i.e., people that own firearms don't want to admit so to a pollster). This is validated by surveys performed by the National Opinion Research Center. They perform their surveys face-to-face at the respondent's home, and routinely have reported gun ownership rates 3-6% lower than telephone based surveys.

[530] Ibid.

[531] This is a serious omission as most gang crime is committed by and against young people.

[532] "*Fear in Britain*," Dr. Paul Gallant and Dr. Joanne Eisen, National Review, July 18, 2000.

were aged below 16. The most reliable measure of crime is that which is reported to the police. We're facing over a million violent crimes a year for the first time in history.[533]

One curious tidbit: Murder rates initially appear to decline after 2002/2003. This is chiefly due to the scores of killings attributed to serial killer, Dr. Harold Frederick Shipman, which were booked in 2002/03 and did not recur in 2003/04.

More curious are the sudden leaps in reported violent crime when the British Home Office enforced standardized methods for recording reported crime (which led the Home Office to claim crime reports to be of poor quality, and thus rely on the suspect survey mechanism):

> The 1998 changes to the Home Office Counting Rules had a very significant impact on violent crime; the numbers of such crimes recorded by the police increased by 83 per cent as a result of the 1998 changes ... The National Crime Recording Standard (NCRS), introduced in April 2002, again resulted in increased recording of violent crimes particularly for less serious violent offences.[534]

ORIGIN OF THE 2ND AMENDMENT

Before the United States Constitution or Bill of Rights existed, most of the thirteen original states had clauses in their constitutions protecting the right to keep and bear arms. When the time came for Congress to draft the Bill of Rights, states submitted clauses from their constitutions that they thought should be added to the Federal Bill of Rights.

Three predominant arms clauses existed at that time (many states had word-for-word copies from other state constitutions and the redundant versions are not mentioned herein).

> Pennsylvania (1776): That *the people have a right to bear arms for the defence of themselves and the state*; and as standing armies in the time of peace are dangerous to liberty, they ought not to be kept up; and that the military should be kept under strict subordination, to, and governed by, the civil power. (Simplified in 1790 to read "The right of the citizens to bear arms in defence of themselves and the State shall not be questioned.")

> Vermont (1777): That *the people have a right to bear arms for the defence of themselves and the State* – and as standing armies in time of peace are dangerous to liberty, they ought not to be kept up; and that the military should be kept under strict subordination to and governed by the civil power.

> Massachusetts (1780): *The people have a right to keep and to bear arms* for the common defence. And as, in time of peace, armies are dangerous to liberty, they ought not to be maintained without the consent of the legislature; and the military power shall always be held in an exact subordination to the civil authority, and be governed by it.

---

[533] "*Row over figures as crime drops 5%,*" David Davis, Shadow Home Secretary, The Guardian, July 22, 2004.

[534] "*Crime in England and Wales 2005/06,*" British Home Office, July 2006.

North Carolina (1776): That *the people have a right to bear arms*, for the defence of the State; and, as standing armies, in time of peace, are dangerous to liberty, they ought not to be kept up; and that the military should be kept under strict subordination to, and governed by, the civil power.

We can see in these state constitution clauses the conjoined purposes as viewed by the people at the time that the 2nd Amendment was drafted.

CALLS FOR THE RIGHT TO KEEP AND BEAR ARMS FROM STATE RATIFICATION CONVENTIONS

Five states that ratified the Constitution sent demands for a Bill of Rights to Congress. All of these demands included a right to keep and bear arms. The relevant parts of these written demands are:

New Hampshire: Twelfth[:] Congress shall never disarm any Citizen unless such as are or have been in Actual Rebellion.

Virginia: …Seventeenth, That *the people have a right to keep and bear arms*; that a well regulated Militia composed of the body of the people trained to arms is the proper, natural and safe defence of a free State. That standing armies in time of peace are dangerous to liberty, and therefore ought to be avoided, as far as the circumstances and protection of the Community will admit; and that in all cases the military should be under strict subordination to and governed by the Civil power.

New York: ... That *the People have a right to keep and bear Arms*; that a well regulated Militia, including the body of the People capable of bearing Arms, is the proper, natural and safe defence of a free State; That the Militia should not be subject to Martial Law except in time of War, Rebellion or Insurrection. That Standing Armies in time of Peace are dangerous to Liberty, and ought not to be kept up, except in Cases of necessity; and that at all times, the Military should be under strict Subordination to the civil Power.

North Carolina: Almost identical to Virginia's demand, but with, "the body of the people, trained to arms," instead of, "the body of the people trained to arms."

Rhode Island: Almost identical to Virginia's demand, but with, "the body of the people capable of bearing arms," instead of, "the body of the people trained to arms," and with a, "militia shall not be subject to martial law," proviso as in New York's.

2ND AMENDMENT DRAFTING, PROPOSALS, AND EDITING

James Madison had the duty of drafting the Bill of Rights from proposed amendments submitted by the states, and most coming from state constitutions. The Bill of Rights went through several revisions. The initial version of the 2nd Amendment read as follows:

> ***The right of the people to keep and bear arms shall not be infringed***; a well armed and well regulated militia being the best security of a free **country**; but no person religiously scrupulous of bearing arms shall be compelled to render military service in person.

The second drafting of the 2nd Amendment saw a rearrangement of the justification and rights clauses, but no change in the intents and purposes therein:

> A well regulated militia, composed of the body of the people,
> being the best security of a free **State**, *the right of the people*
> *to keep and bear arms shall not be infringed*, but no person
> religiously scrupulous shall be compelled to bear arms.

Notice that in the original draft, Madison used the phrase "free country" as the object of what is protected by the militia. In subsequent drafts, the word "state" was substituted. This is important because the concept of "state" and "country" are interchangeable, whereas "state*s*" (plural) and "country" are not. Throughout the rest of the Constitution, when the states and their powers were defined, the plural was always used but in the 2nd Amendment it was not. Clearly, the intent of militia protection defined in the 2nd Amendment was to protect a form of government, not define the power of the several states.

Four further revisions removed objectionable concepts (such as the "conscientious objector" clause). On September 9, 1789, a member of the Senate proposed adding "for the common defense" onto the draft of the Second Amendment. In other words, the proposed wording of the amendment would have read:

> A well regulated militia being the security of a free State, the
> right of the people to bear arms *for the common defense*, shall
> not be infringed.

The proposed change was <u>voted down</u>. This is instructive because some believe that the current wording of the amendment exists specifically for collective/common/mutual defense, and has no bearing on individual self defense. However, the Senate considered adding this restriction and rejected it.

It is clear from these origins and first drafts, and from contemporary commentaries on the clause, that the original intent was to secure an individual right. The commentaries of St. George Tucker (The American Blackstone) and Supreme Court Justice Joseph Story, both of whom were federal jurists and chronologically close to the authoring of the amendment, bear this out.

ARMS CLAUSES OF STATES THAT JOINED SHORTLY AFTER THE 2ND AMENDMENT WAS RATIFIED

Also worth review are arms clauses in the constitutions of states that joined the Union shortly <u>after</u> ratification of the Bill of Rights. These demonstrate the contemporary understanding of the amendment and the rights of the people:

Kentucky (1792): That *the right of the citizens to bear arms in defense of themselves* and the State shall not be questioned.

Tennessee (1796): That the freemen of this State have a right to keep and to bear arms for their common defence.

Kentucky (1799): That *the rights of the citizens to bear arms in defense of themselves* and the State shall not be questioned.

Ohio (1802): That *the people have a right to bear arms for the defence of themselves* and the State; and as standing armies, in time of peace, are dangerous to liberty, they shall not be kept up, and that the military shall be kept under strict subordination to the civil power.

Indiana (1816): That *the people have a right to bear arms for the defense of themselves* and the State, and that the military shall be kept in strict subordination to the civil power.

Mississippi (1817): *Every citizen has a right to bear arms, in defence of himself* and the State.

Connecticut (1818): *Every citizen has a right to bear arms in defense of himself* and the state.

Maine (1819): Every citizen has a right to keep and bear arms for the common defence; and this right shall never be questioned.

Alabama (1819): That *every citizen has a right to bear arms in defence of himself* and the state.

Missouri (1820): That the people have the right peaceably to assemble for their commongood, and to apply to those vested with the powers of government for redress of grievances by petition or remonstrance; and that their *right to bear arms in defence of themselves* and of the State cannot be questioned.

Made in the USA
Lexington, KY
06 January 2015